RON HAAS

ASK FOR A FISH

BOLD, FAITH-BASED FUNDRAISING

Cover Design: Sarah P. Merrill
Interior Design: Michelle VanGeest
Cartoon Illustrations: Ron Wheeler

ISBN 0-9788585-3-0

Printed in the United States of America

Special Thanks

To Cynthia,
who said "Yes!" when I asked.
"A good woman is hard to find,
and worth far more than diamonds."
(Prov. 31:10–11, The Message)

To three friends
who opened my eyes to generous giving:

Bob Cone,
who gave me a chance to learn fundraising
from the other side of the desk,

Arch Bonnema,
who inspired me to excel in the
grace of giving (2 Cor. 8:7),

and

Pat McLaughlin,
who taught me how to ask.

CONTENTS

INTRODUCTION

Learning to Ask for a Fish

"Give a man a fish; you have fed him for today.
Teach a man to fish;
and you have fed him for a lifetime."
– Author unknown

Fundraising is sometimes described as "fishing" for donors, but the fishing metaphor is misleading. Real fishermen bait their fish into making bad decisions. Fundraisers might strategize about "fishing in the right ponds," "choosing the right donor hook," or "reeling in a huge catch." They might even tell fish stories about "the big one" they landed, or even "the one that got away." But these images wrongly imply that fundraising *the!* means luring someone into doing something they will eventually regret. Instead of fishing, a better analogy for fundraising can be seen in Jesus' lesson about prayer:

7

"So I say to you: Ask and it will be given to you; seek and you will find; knock and the door will be opened to you. For everyone who asks receives; the one who seeks finds; and to the one who knocks, the door will be opened. Which of you fathers, if your son asks for a fish, will give him a snake instead? Or if he asks for an egg, will give him a scorpion? If you then, though you are evil, know how to give good gifts to your children, how much more will your Father in heaven give the Holy Spirit to those who ask him!" (Luke 11:9–13)

must 1st ask God!

In every successful fundraising effort, asking is the key. The first "ask" must be to ask God for his blessing. Nothing of significance for eternity can be accomplished without prayer. Jesus taught us to boldly approach the throne of grace and plead with God for our needs. Jesus illustrates the principle of asking our heavenly Father for what we need by using an earthly picture of a son asking his father for a fish. If we as sinful humans can give good gifts to our children, by comparison God the Father can bless us with great gifts—if we only ask!

Bill Bright of Campus Crusade was perhaps the most successful Christian fundraiser in modern times. Few Christian leaders have equaled his ability to cultivate relationships with major donors and challenge them to make significant gifts. David Hubbard, longtime president of Fuller Theological Seminary, once complained, "Whenever I go and meet a wealthy person, I find that Bill Bright has been there first."[1]

Bill was a visionary with God-sized dreams that required God-sized resources. In the late 1970s, Here's Life, World, was Campus Crusade's plan to reach a billion people with the gospel. Bill calculated that it would cost $1 per individual gospel presentation, which meant that he needed to raise $1 billion. His first thought was to ask a million donors to give $1,000, but then he realized that the only way to turn his dream into reality would be to ask one thousand donors to each give $1 million. Bill's major donors became known as "History's Handful."

The JESUS film was Campus Crusade's most successful tool for global evangelism. Crusade divided the world into one thousand "Million People Target Areas." For example, of Jamaica's three million residents, an estimated two million had been exposed to the gospel, so one million people were still unreached. Major donors were challenged to make million-dollar commitments to underwrite an evangelistic effort for a specific target area.

> "History's Handful" achieved the holy grail of fundraising: "donor buy-in."

In the mid 1990s, businessmen became evangelists for the JESUS film fundraising effort. Arch Bonnema, a Texas entrepreneur, took the responsibility for Jamaica, but he didn't just write a check. Arch made fifty-four trips to Jamaica in sixty months and took more than 550 friends with him to partner with JESUS film teams. These vision trips were life changing. For many of Arch's friends, this was the first mission trip they had ever taken. College seniors, business executives, pastors, families, and newly retired senior citizens experienced evangelism first-hand. Donors caught the vision and would say, "If Arch and Sherry can do this, we can do this!" Ninety percent of those who went to Jamaica later took another mission trip. Many signed up to sponsor a crusade in another part of the world and flew off to encourage their JESUS film team.

Some of the businessmen who got involved were nationals from the countries where the JESUS film had been shown. A donor in Jamaica underwrote the teams in Guatemala and Haiti. Another donor in Mexico sponsored teams in other parts of Mexico. Major donors all over the world got involved. Every year these businessmen-evangelists would meet to share their stories about what God was accomplishing in "their" country and strategize about how to encourage more people to give and go. The atmosphere was like a high-energy sales conference for a multi-level marketing company! Donors got fired up and left with a renewed zeal to go out and reach the world for Christ.

"History's Handful" achieved the holy grail of fundraising: "donor buy-in." Bill Bright cast the vision for actually fulfilling the Great Commission, and donors gave because the story was so compelling. Through the impact of the JESUS film, millions of people made decisions for Christ. "History's Handful" worked because donors got personally involved. The meetings weren't run by staff members who gave reports about what *they* were doing on the field. Instead, donors testified how God was using them to spread the gospel. Major donors weren't just giving money to send someone else; they were buying plane tickets to the front lines. "History's Handful" accomplished an incredible fundraising goal because friends asked friends to give. There is nothing more powerful than peer-to-peer fundraising.

Jesus' picture of a son asking his father for a fish teaches us to ask our heavenly Father for what we need, but we can also apply this asking principle to our human relationships. If we want someone to support our ministry's vision with their time, treasure, and talent, we've got to ask. Asking, seeking, and knocking on heaven's door seems easy. We all understand the basics of prayer. Our problem with prayer isn't that we don't know what to do; it's that we aren't serious enough about it. When it comes to fundraising, the steps seem a little fuzzier. Whom do I talk to? What do I say? How much should I ask for? What if they turn me down? Do I really have to ask?

This book outlines seven action steps for bold, faith-based fundraising:

	Action Step 1: **Pray**	Raising money for Christian endeavors must be a spiritual activity for the asker and the donor.
	Action Step 2: **Give**	You must give a generous, sacrificial gift before you can ask others to support your ministry.
	Action Step 3: **Network**	Fundraising is not about what you know but who you know.
	Action Step 4: **Invite**	The most effective way to build a donor base is one friend at a time.
	Action Step 5: **Ask**	Perhaps the most fearful step of all is to ask someone for money.
	Action Step 6: **Work**	Nothing's easy! Successful fundraising requires relentless patience and hard work.
	Action Step 7: **Thank**	It doesn't cost much to say thanks, but it might cost a lot if you forget to do it.

Each chapter concludes with a testimony about the joys of generous giving and the joys of asking, as well as group discussion helps for you and your board.

Fundraising isn't really about fishing; it's about learning to ask for a fish!

ACTION STEP 1: PRAY

Ask and It Will Be Given to You

Why start a book about fundraising by talking about prayer? Sure, we believe God owns the cattle on a thousand hills, but are we serious about asking him to supply our ministry's needs? Does prayer take a primary role in your fundraising efforts? We want God to guide our strategic-planning process, but when it comes to fundraising, we might be tempted to "lean on our own understanding" by attending the latest seminar, reading about the best practices of highly successful fundraisers, or even listening to our favorite consultant. It's so easy to jump into a discussion about fundraising strategy and tactics and not even mention prayer. By starting our fundraising plan with prayer, we acknowledge that our success is completely in God's hands. Given the two options of a great strategy or passionate prayer, the best path is to "Trust in the Lord" (Prov. 3:5).

Jesus taught his disciples to pray, "Father, hallowed be your name, your kingdom come. Give us each day our daily bread" (Luke 11:2–3). If we should ask our heavenly Father to supply our daily bread as individuals, then as an organization why not pray that he would give us our daily budget? I know you believe in prayer, but are you bold?

> *"Pray as though everything depended on God. Work as though everything depended on you."*
> ST. AUGUSTINE

Then Jesus said to them, "Suppose you have a friend, and you go to him at midnight and say, 'Friend, lend me three loaves of bread; a friend of mine on a journey has come to me, and I have no food to offer him.' And suppose the one inside answers, 'Don't bother me. The door is already locked, and my children and I are in bed. I can't get up and give you anything.' I tell you, even though he will not get up and give you the bread because of friendship, yet because of your shameless audacity he will surely get up and give you as much as you need.

"So I say to you: Ask and it will be given to you; seek and you will find; knock and the door will be opened to you. For everyone who asks receives; the one who seeks finds; and to the one who knocks, the door will be opened." (Luke 11:5–10)

Boldly Asking God for Help

This parable feels uncomfortable because it seems to teach that we must pester God or he won't pay attention to us. The man was annoyed because his needy friend had the gall to bang on his door at midnight. His initial response was, "Go away. Leave me alone. Your problems are not my problems."

Maybe we don't ask God to solve our financial woes because we don't want to bother him. Or maybe we think we can solve our problems by ourselves, but we can't.

The man finally got out of bed because of his friend's "shameless audacity." The friend just wouldn't give up. He kept knocking and asking until he got the answer he wanted. God wants us to beg him to respond to our desperate situation. It's not that he's too busy to be bothered or that he is unconcerned about our needs. He wants us to learn total dependence upon him. This kind of serious prayer is hard work. Jacob wrestled with the Lord through the night and would not let go until the Lord blessed him (see Gen. 32:22–31). Paul's fellow laborer, Epaphras, was "always wrestling in prayer" (Col. 4:12) for the church in Collossae. Nehemiah fasted and prayed for four months for the desperate situation of those living in Jerusalem before God gave him the plan and resources to move forward (see Neh. 1:1–11). How would your ministry be transformed if you prayed with this kind of intensity? *whoa ... true!*

Praying in the Money

George Müeller proved that, "The prayer of a righteous person is powerful and effective" (James 5:16). God led him to establish the Ashley Down orphanage in Bristol, England, which cared for more than ten thousand orphans during his lifetime. Müeller's fundraising plan was simply to pray, "The first and primary object of the work was [and still is] that God might be magnified by the fact that the orphans under my care are provided with all they need, only by prayer and faith without anyone being asked by me or my fellow-laborers whereby it may be seen, that God is FAITHFUL, STILL, AND HEARS PRAYER STILL."[2]

Müeller was convicted that he should avoid any method that could appear to be self-serving or manipulative. He re-

Be the mission of charity!

fused to ask anyone for money. He was completely silent about the needs of his orphanages—he made no public appeals, or- *whon...* ganized no fundraising events, mailed no letters, distributed no brochures, and printed no annual reports. "Through grace we had learned to lean upon the Lord only, being assured, that, if we were never to speak or write one single word more about this work, yet should we be supplied with means, as long as He should enable us to depend on Himself alone. . . . What better proof, therefore, could we give of our depending

> "He may not get up and give you the bread, just because you are his friend. But he will get up and give you as much as you need, simply because you are not ashamed to keep on asking" (LUKE 11:8 CEV).

upon the living God alone, and not upon public meetings or printed reports?"[3] Müeller's testimony of answered prayer is truly remarkable.

Shameless, Audacious Asking

The apostle Paul took another approach to raising money. In 2 Corinthians 8 and 9, he wrote to the Corinthian church about the dire straits of the church in Jerusalem and then unashamedly encouraged them to "excel in this grace of giving" (2 Cor. 8:7). Paul even tested the sincerity of their love by "comparing it with the earnestness of others" (2 Cor. 8:8). He was fearless when he sent Titus and the brothers to make sure that the Corinthians' gift would be ready in time (see 8:16–24). The Corinthian believers testified of their love for God, but Paul challenged them to "prove it" by giving a generous gift. Incredibly he said, "Show these men the proof of your love" (8:24).

Paul wasn't shy about talking about money. He instructed Timothy to "Command those who are rich in this present world not to be arrogant nor to put their hope in wealth, which is so uncertain, but to put their hope in God, who richly provides us with everything for our enjoyment. Command them to do good, to be rich in good deeds, and to be generous and willing to share" (1 Tim. 6:17–18). If you are uncomfortable with the impudence of the friend at midnight, how do you feel about Paul's charge to "command" people to be generous? Paul was a man of prayer who asked God boldly, and he also boldly asked others to give generously.

[margin note: be rave to share what you have or His kingdom]

How can we reconcile praying silently with shameless, audacious asking? St. Augustine probably couldn't have imagined modern fundraising, but his famous quote has a direct application: "Pray as though everything depended on God. Work as though everything depended on you." Prayer must be your primary fundraising task, but there are at least two key steps you can take to gather the resources your ministry desperately needs: (a) you can speak and write about how God is using your ministry to impact lives, and (b) you can openly ask people to partner with you.

[margin note: (a) speak/write about your work (b) openly ask people to join mission]

Boldly Asking Your Friends for Help

The Friend at Midnight parable teaches us to be persistent in prayer. God wants us to boldly approach the throne of grace so we can "find grace to help us in our time of need" (Heb. 4:16). But this parable also offers some practical applications for asking our friends for help. Many non-profit board members get queasy when it comes to fundraising—especially if it involves asking their own friends for money. "I know our ministry needs money, but I can't ask my friends because it might harm our friendship."

Mark Twain captured this inner fear in his book *Pudd'nhead Wilson's Calendar*: "The holy passion of Friendship is of so sweet and steady and loyal and enduring a nature that it will last through a whole lifetime, if not asked to lend money." Asking for a gift is even tougher than asking for a loan. The fear is reasonable. We are all sinners, and conversations about money have strained more than one friendship. Board members tend to take three approaches toward friends with money. Some are fearless and will ask anybody for anything, anytime. Others are willing to share names as long as the source is not revealed, but won't ask. The rest either don't know anybody with money or are afraid to point out people with money in the crowd.

Let's take a closer look at this late-night donor visit between two friends to discover seven fundraising applications.

1. The man faced a desperate need.

Why couldn't this man wait until morning? What was the compelling reason he needed three loaves of bread right then? Was his request made so he could save face with his guest? That seems a little shallow. Perhaps his visitor had just arrived from a long journey and hadn't eaten in days. Perhaps he had small children who were crying from hunger or an elderly family member who was weak or sick. Whatever the situation, this man asked his friend because he couldn't solve the problem by himself. You probably can't write a personal check to accomplish all your ministry goals. What problems could you solve if you only had more resources? Who won't be reached if you can't move forward with your plans? What essential programs won't be accomplished without help? Why should a donor make a significant gift to your ministry? How desperate are you? *so true ... how badly do we want to do more in the ministry?*

18

2. The hour was late.

It was midnight—not an ideal time to make a donor call. Rudeness and obnoxiousness are not usually desirable character traits for development professionals. However, some people are so fearful about offending a friend that they never bring up the subject of money, even in broad daylight! By going at midnight this man proved how motivated he was to provide for his guest. This was urgent. Successful fundraisers have passion to do whatever it takes to meet the need. If you're a board member who is not passionate enough about your cause to ask your friends for money, maybe you should question whether or not you should continue serving on the board. Effective board members are willing to give and to get others to give, even if it's inconvenient.

> ✳ "Prayer is my first advice. Prayer is my second suggestion. And prayer is my third suggestion."
> DR. BILLY KIM

3. The man was asking to benefit someone else.

Some executive directors struggle with asking because a portion of the gift will cover their salary. They stumble over a mental block because it feels like they are asking for their own benefit. It's proper for non-profit organizations to pay their staff members. "The worker deserves his wages" (1 Tim. 5:18). Assuming that your salary isn't exorbitant, it's completely legitimate to ask for a gift. The man in this parable probably enjoyed a piece of bread with his guest, but the reason he asked for the bread was to benefit his guest, not himself. The same goes for every ministry fundraiser. The reason you ask for money is so that your ministry has enough resources to provide the programs that change lives. Keep yourself focused on the people who would be lost were it not for your ministry's impact. As a fundraiser you must avoid the love of money at all costs, because "Some people, eager for money, have wandered from the faith and pierced themselves with many griefs" (1 Tim. 6:10). *all that you recieve is a gift from God! Not yours anyway...*

4. The man turned to his friend for help.

If God called you to the mission field, who would you ask for prayer and financial support? The man in this parable asked his friend for help. He didn't approach a total stranger; he went to the person with whom he had cultivated a close relationship. Many executive directors have reality show fantasies of an *all about relati'!* anonymous mega-donor knocking on the door with a big smile and a big cardboard check. They'll have to keep dreaming. People give to people they know and trust. A generous donor in California has a vision to develop hospitals in third world countries. His strategy is, "I don't have enough money to build these by myself, so I have to get my friends to help me." A true friend will answer a midnight phone call.

5. The man wouldn't listen to excuses.

People make lots of excuses for not being generous. Some excuses are legitimate, most are not. The friend in this parable was no exception. He had a laundry list of reasons for why he couldn't give. "The door is already locked, and my children and I are in bed. I can't get up and give you anything." Today's donors also have a list of ready excuses for why they can't give you anything. "It's an inconvenient time." "I'm focused on other things." "I've got my money locked up in something else." Countless circumstances stand in the way of generosity. The bottom line for the man in our story was simply, "I can't." Notice that he didn't say, "I don't have anything to give you." This man had the capacity to give; he just wasn't motivated. It wasn't a matter of "I can't" but "I don't want to." That didn't deter our friend, and it shouldn't slow you down, either. You can't make anyone give, but you can pray boldly that God would compel them. *Whoa... Fortitude + Stamina!*

6. His friend gave because the man kept asking.

The interesting fundraising application from this parable is that the friend didn't give just because he was a friend, which goes against all we know about friendship fundraising. "He may not get up and give you the bread, just because you are his friend. But he will get up and give you as much as you need, simply because you are not ashamed to keep on asking" (Luke 11:8 CEV). Asking is the key. Friendship might get you in the door, but asking gets a gift. How many times should you call? A donor representative recently made six attempts to catch a prospect on the phone. On the seventh time, the donor answered, and they had a wonderful two-hour phone call. Most people give up too early. Persistence pays.

7. Asking impacts the donor's entire family.

The friend gave a plausible excuse for not giving. He had tucked everyone into bed and didn't want to bother. To give the bread, he would have to get up, light a lamp, rustle around—and there was a good chance that he would wake the baby. This was not a do-it-quick and then-jump-back-into-bed transaction. It could take a couple of hours to calm everybody down. In the same way, some gifts can create a ruckus with a donor's family. Asking for a six- or seven-figure gift probably impacts the *whole* family. Mom or Dad might be giving away a part of their children's inheritance, and someone might cry foul. Should that prevent you from asking? It didn't stop our friend at midnight, and it shouldn't stop you.

Fine-Tuning Your Boldness Meter

All this talk about boldness might cause some people to crank up the intensity a little too high. A prominent female major donor has noted that in the past few years she has been getting phone calls, letters, and personal visits from ministry directors and development staff who literally demand that she give a gift to their organization. They don't ask, "Would you consider a gift of $50,000?" or "Would you pray about giving a gift of $100,000?" Their actual words are, "You *must* give a gift of $250,000 to this project." That's not biblical boldness; it's just plain rude.

One major donor enrolled his children in a new school. Thirty days later the headmaster of the school showed up at his door and asked for a $25,000 gift. The major donor asked, "Do you promote premarital sex at your school?" "Absolutely not," replied the headmaster. The donor continued, "Asking for a major gift so quickly is kind of like having sex before marriage. You should slow down a little so you can get to know our family. Let's wait and see how my kids adjust to the school, and then we can talk about my financial involvement." Boldness and brashness are two different things.

Another generous major donor experienced a similar abrupt attitude from a development director who said, "God has blessed you with this big house, and you've got lots money. You ought to give to our ministry." How presumptuous and arrogant. This fundraising attitude will make your donors feel like they would if a vacuum salesman dumped a bag of dirt all over their white carpet for no apparent reason. We should treat donors in the same way Peter asks us to answer seekers, "with gentleness and respect" (1 Peter 3:15).

Hopefully, these bad examples are the exception, not the rule. The vast majority of Christian fundraisers will swing toward the "Minnesota nice" side of the pendulum and approach donors in a courteous, reserved, and mild-mannered way. We must approach donors in a Christ-honoring way with a love that is patient, kind, not proud, and not self-seeking.

Everyone Who Asks Receives

Jesus concludes his parable of the friend at midnight with three commands: keep on asking, keep on seeking, and keep on knocking, because by relentlessly pursuing the answer to your needs you will receive, you will find, and the door will be opened to you.

So you must ask God boldly, and you must also boldly ask your friends. God can supply your needs, but you must cry out to him. Your friends might not give just because they are your friends, but they might give "simply because you are not ashamed to keep on asking" (Luke 11:8 CEV). Be bold, but be gracious!

The Other Rick Warren—Fundraising Fire

It's no coincidence that Rick Warren, a businessman who owns a copper and aluminum forging company, is also a man of passionate prayer. "The prayer of a righteous person is powerful and effective" (James 5:16). Forging is a process where metal is preheated to a desired temperature and then pressed, pounded, or squeezed under great pressure into high-strength parts. God has pressed, pounded, and squeezed Rick through several personal trials to bring him to genuine faith in Jesus Christ. God continues to mold Rick into his image through the power of prayer. Rick serves as a board member for several Christian organizations and has experienced what it means to trust God for one's daily budget.

Rick, what role does prayer play in your service as a board member?

During my first year on one particular board, our ministry faced a series of incredible challenges. We had financial problems, leadership issues, struggles with our enrollment, facility challenges, and even serious questions about whether or not we could survive. Our meetings were just terrible. We would hash and rehash issues but never seemed to make progress. Then we decided to commit ourselves to prayer. We devoted an entire meeting to prayer. It didn't happen overnight, but God began to answer our prayers in unbelievable ways. The impact on our meetings was dramatic. Before we started getting serious about prayer, our meetings would last for hours and not accomplish much. After we started focusing on prayer, our meetings were often finished in half the time and were marked by unity and wisdom. Prayer made all the difference.

How does prayer impact your fundraising effort?

It all starts with prayer. We must share our ministry with people and ask them to give, but if we don't spend time in prayer, we usually just go through the motions and don't accomplish much. I am involved in the spiritual emphasis committee of a capital campaign attempting to raise millions of dollars. We pray for God to help us identify potential donors and open doors so that we can share our story. We need to realize that this ministry is God's ministry, and he wants it to succeed more than we do. I've challenged each member of our capital campaign steering committee to encourage their subcommittees and departments to commit themselves to serious prayer. We pray for specific requests, but we spend most of our time just praising God for who he is.

What role does prayer play in your personal giving decisions?

This might sound strange, but I don't usually struggle in prayer over a giving decision. I feel like the Holy Spirit is guiding all of my decisions in life. So when God puts a giving opportunity on my heart, generally I don't resist an impulse to give.

What is God teaching you about prayer?

Recently, I had the privilege of traveling to South Korea to visit several ministries. One of the highlights of my trip was meeting pastor-evangelist Billy Kim. In 1960, he started Suwon Central Baptist Church with ten members. He served forty-five years as pastor and saw the membership grow to more than fifteen thousand. Dr. Kim is also the chairman of the Far East Broadcasting Company—Korea, a network of eleven radio stations that broadcast into China, Russia, Japan, and Korea. When I asked Dr. Kim what he attributed to his church's phenomenal growth, he said, "We hold a 4:15 a.m. prayer service every day at my church that attracts two thousand people and overflows the church's main sanctuary."

A few years ago I attended a conference where Dr. Kim shared his amazing testimony. Early in his ministry, he attended a church growth seminar in Japan and asked a fellow pastor, "Why is it that on Sunday morning you have five hundred thousand people rushing to hear you preach, but my church has only about ten thousand people?" The pastor asked, "How long are you praying every day?" Dr. Kim said, "About thirty to forty minutes," to which his friend replied, "I pray five hours a day." Later Dr. Kim reflected on that conversation, "I have no question that when a man prays five hours a day, God will begin to use that man."

I read that Billy Kim once challenged some seminary students by saying, "Prayer is my first advice. Prayer is my second suggestion. And prayer is my third suggestion." I was humbled to meet such a man of God and realized that if our ministry wants to experience the same kind of blessings, we need to get more serious about prayer.

How would you respond to board members who say, "Our job is to make sure this ministry stays on track spiritually; we aren't here to raise money"?

Serving on a non-profit board is different than serving as an elder in your church. Elders care the spiritual concerns of a congregation, while deacons focus on the physical and financial issues. Non-profit board members face unique agenda items like casting a vision, recruiting the right team, putting out fires, responding to external threats, and making sure the organization stays true to their mission. Perhaps the greatest challenge a non-profit board faces is finding enough resources to adequately fund their ministry's vision. Some board members shy away from fundraising, because they view it as a secular means to a spiritual end. I believe in the power of prayer, and I also believe that board members must tell their ministry's story to as many people as possible. Part of your job as a board member is keeping your ministry on target, but an equally important part of your job is fundraising.

How would you encourage board members to be more effective?

I would totally challenge them about their commitment to prayer. Being a person of prayer should be the main qualification for selecting a board member. Once a board member joins a board, they should allocate a significant amount of time praying for their ministry. In fact, I would choose a praying board member over a successful businessman any day of the week. One of the most effective board members I know is a woman who doesn't know much about business, finance, or education, but she knows how to pray. When I have a problem, I give Ruth a call and ask her to pray. Some boards choose members who have lots of money or a great reputation, but I am happy to have Ruth because as a prayer warrior she is my go-to board member.

Action Step 1: Pray

Group Discussion

1. **Our corporate prayer life can be characterized as:**
   - ❏ Stone Cold
   - ❏ Cool Ashes
   - ❏ Burning Embers
   - ❏ Raging Fire

2. **How can we strengthen our board commitment to prayer and fasting?**

   _____

   _____

   _____

3. **How can we pray more specifically for our ministry leaders, staff, and those we serve?**

   _____

   _____

   _____

4. **How can we encourage our key donors to pray with us?**

   _____

   _____

   _____

5. **How can we foster a climate of prayer throughout our organization?**

   _____

   _____

   _____

Personal Reflection

In the next month, can I commit to a four-hour block of time to pray for this ministry?

ACTION STEP 2: GIVE

Skin in the Game

Investment guru Warren Buffett coined the phrase "skin in the game" to describe a situation in which high-ranking insiders use their own money to buy stock in the company they are running. Buffett believes that when managers share a stake in the company, they are more interested in the company's success. Executives can say they believe in their company, but talk is cheap. Buffett wants them to prove it by putting their own money on the line just like outside investors do.

Having "skin in the game" actually just expresses a biblical principle: "For where your treasure is, there your heart will be also" (Matt. 6:21). We say, "Put your money where your mouth is." But we should say, "Put your money where your heart is." If you are an executive director, staff member, or board member, you should give generously to the ministry in which you serve.

If you, as a high-ranking insider, don't believe enough in what you are doing to support it financially, how can you credibly ask outsiders to give?

When David gathered resources for the temple, he gave first out of his own personal wealth and then asked the elders to give before he involved the congregation. David didn't just give a token amount; he set the pace with a generous gift of three thousand talents of gold. Today, we measure gold in ounces, which makes David's gift a whopping 3,520,000 ounces. Depending on the daily spot gold prices of our time, David's gift was worth around $6 billion—that's billion. David also threw in another $266 million in silver, just for good measure.

> We say, "Put your money where your mouth is." But we should say, "Put your money where your heart is."

David's leadership gift inspired the elders, and they stepped up with another $8.7 billion in gold, plus $389 million in silver, 675 tons of bronze, 3,800 tons of iron, and precious jewels of every kind. What a way to kick off a campaign! Their enthusiasm spread throughout the whole congregation. "The people rejoiced at the willing response of their leaders, for they had given freely and wholeheartedly to the LORD" (1 Chron. 29:9).

Some Common Excuses

People who don't give blood offer several lame excuses. "Others are giving enough." "I don't have any spare blood to donate." "My blood isn't rich enough." "They'll take too much and I'll feel weak." And the old standby, "I'm too busy." People who don't want to give money also have a list of excuses. They might not say them out loud, but the little voice in their head feeds them one or more of these lines to keep them from giving.

"I'm Not a Wealthy Person"

Very few of us could give $6 billion like David, but even if you don't have the capacity to give a leadership gift, you can still give a generous gift. The early church in Jerusalem was facing a severe crisis, so Paul organized a relief effort and asked the churches in Asia Minor for help. When he presented the opportunity to the churches in Macedonia, something amazing happened. These believers, who were in great need themselves, responded with an incredible gift. Their generosity surprised Paul so much that he was reluctant to take it, but they insisted. Paul wrote, "In the midst of a very severe trial, their overflowing joy and their extreme poverty welled up in rich generosity. For I testify that they gave as much as they were able, and even beyond their ability" (2 Cor. 8:2–3).

How do you give "beyond your ability"? We view generous giving from the perspective of how much we can afford. The Macedonian believers were motivated by the compelling need and their desire to obey God, which shows that generosity is not necessarily connected to a person's net worth. Jesus observed that even though the Pharisees gave lots of money, the widow gave more generously with her two small copper coins because, "They all gave out of their wealth; but she, out of her poverty, put in everything—all she had to live on" (Mark 12:44). Don't listen to the little voice in your head that tells you that you can't give anything. Maybe you're not rich, but you can experience "rich generosity."

"If I Had It, I'd Give It"

A generous donor tried and tried to encourage his friend to give. His friend had the money and even expressed an interest in giving, but he always had a business excuse that held him back. He would say, "I'm on the verge of this big deal that will put me over the top. I want to give, but I need the money right now. When this hits, I'll be able to give much more." Sadly, this person never got around to giving, because his money was always tied up chasing the next deal. Giving should be based upon what you have, not on what you wish you had. Maybe you've said, "If I had a million dollars, I'd give it." Paul's instruction to the Corinthians teaches an important principle: "The gift is acceptable according to what one has, not according to what one does not have" (2 Cor. 8:12). Those who wait to give until they can afford to give are still waiting to give.

"I Give My Time Instead"

Volunteer time is a valuable commodity. In 2011, 64.3 million Americans volunteered almost eight billion hours for an estimated value of roughly $171 billion. The Corporation for National and Community Service has calculated that the value of volunteer time for 2011 was $21.79 per hour.[4] Time is valuable, but it's not a substitute for generous financial giving. We should give our "time, talent, and treasure," not our "time *or* talent *or* treasure."

A new believer asked a deacon how he determined what to give. The deacon responded, "I add up all the time I spend serving and deduct it from my tithe." This attitude reflects an accounting approach to giving but forgets that God is the one who balances the books. "Remember this: Whoever sows sparingly will also reap sparingly, and whoever sows generously will also reap generously" (2 Cor. 9:6).

Why do people use the "I give my time instead" excuse? Is it because they really don't have the money, or is it because they perceive that giving time doesn't cost them anything? David understood the importance of giving something of value. Near the end of his life, he sinned by taking a census of his fighting men (see 2 Samuel 24). The only way to stop God's judgment was to offer a sacrifice, so David asked to purchase Araunah's threshing floor to build an altar. Araunah offered his property as a gift, but David insisted on paying full price for the land, declaring, "I will not sacrifice to the LORD my God burnt offerings that cost me nothing" (v. 24). David wanted to demonstrate his love for the Lord by giving something of value. He was not willing to take credit for someone else's sacrificial gift.

The "I give my time instead" excuse sounds a little like the "faith versus works" argument from James: "But someone will say, 'You have faith; I have deeds.' Show me your faith without deeds, and I will show you my faith by my deeds" (James 2:18). Let me paraphrase and put it in the context of giving: "But someone will say, 'I give time, you give money.' Give your time without money, and I will give my time and my money." Giving time and money should not be an either/or option, but a both/and action. After all, the ministry you serve can't pay the electric bill with your time.

"But I Serve on Several Other Boards"

Effective board members are in high demand and some are recruited for multiple boards. One board member keeps track of his board responsibilities on a spreadsheet that now totals more than thirty-five nonprofit organizations. He limits himself to ten to twelve active board assignments, but even then it's difficult to see how he can effectively serve that many ministries. Just showing up at all the board meetings is a full-time job, then there's the issue of potential conflicts of interests. No doubt, he is a talented individual, but it's doubtful that he has a big red "S" on his chest. When asked to contribute a leadership gift to one of the organizations, he declined based upon all his other commitments. If it's hard to give to multiple organizations, it's even harder to ask for money. Can you imagine his conversation with any potential donor? "Today, I'm here to ask you to support ABC Ministries. I'll be back next week to talk with you about XYZ Ministries."

The Parable of the Good Board Member

The Good Samaritan parable provides some interesting applications for board members. It starts with a conversation between Jesus and a lawyer who questioned, "What must I do to inherit eternal life?" (Luke 10:25). Jesus asked him what the Law said, to which the man replied to love God and love others. At this point, the lawyer began to justify himself with the question, "Who is my neighbor?" (10:29). He was looking for the minimum standard requirement for pleasing God, but Jesus responded with a story of a person who went far beyond what was expected of him.

You remember the parable: A man was traveling from Jerusalem to Jericho and was ambushed by thieves who stripped him, beat him, and left him for dead. A priest walked by, but instead of stopping to help, he moved to the other side of the road. A Levite walked by, but he also went out of his way to avoid the situation. Then a Samaritan on a business trip saw the man's plight and took pity on him. He bandaged his wounds, put the man on his donkey, and took him to an inn to care for him. The next morning he gave the innkeeper the equivalent of two day's wages and asked him to look after the man until he returned. This incredible story illustrates at least five qualities of effective board members.

1. Compassion

The Samaritan's heart was moved to action. This is where ministry starts; something inside this man went out to this poor individual who was hurting. In stark contrast, the priest and Levite saw the man but walked right on by. Evidently they had more important things to do with their time. Board members are busy people, so most find time to serve out of a heart of compassion for their fellow man. What prompted you to join a board? What's the compelling reason that causes you to invest time in serving others? Some boards are populated by "obit" members, people who are motivated by the "praise of men" and only serve prestigious organizations to build their obituary resumes. Effective board members are moved by the ministry's mission and vision. They are willing to put their shoulder to the plow

> "No one would remember the Good Samaritan if he'd only had good intentions; he had money as well."
> MARGARET THATCHER

and do whatever it takes to advance the cause. It's a heart issue.

2. Time Commitment

Helping others requires a great investment of time. The Good Samaritan took a whole day out of his schedule to reach out to this man. Giving a homeless person a few dollars takes a minute, and might not be the best way to truly help that person, but this poor man was in trauma and needed both immediate and long-term care. A quick fix wasn't going to solve his problem. One of the greatest challenges of recruiting board members is finding candidates who are willing to invest the time. According to BoardSource, the average board member spends 15.9 hours per month on board work, plus attending special events, volunteering, or providing some in-kind or pro-bono professional services.[5] One challenge many boards face is that some people might agree to join the board but then rarely attend meetings. When you sign up to take on the task, you must count the cost.

3. Personal Interest

The victim was lying in the ditch beaten to a pulp. The parable says the Samaritan "went to him and bandaged his wounds, pouring on oil and wine" (10:34). The word *pouring* indicates lavishness and generosity. He didn't just dab a little wine and oil here and there and call it good; he lavishly poured out the antiseptic to cleanse the wound and emptied out an abundance of oil to soothe the man's pain. Perhaps he tore part of his garment into bandages to wrap the wounds. This was hands-on ministry. There was no way to help this man without getting blood stains on his own robe. Think of the care he showed as he gently lifted the man onto his donkey. Then he slowly took him to the inn where he cared for him during the night. Being a board member requires an intense personal interest in serving people. You can't lead from an ivory tower; you have to get in the trenches with people and help heal their broken lives. Taking a casual approach just doesn't cut it.

4. Generosity

Here's where the story connects to giving. This mission of mercy cost the Samaritan in several ways. His first gift was in opportunity costs; perhaps he missed his scheduled appointment and a possible financial gain. But beyond that, he used his personal supply of wine and oil to care for the man. He might have sacrificed the clothing he was wearing to fashion makeshift bandages. He also had cash-out-of-pocket expenses when he gave the innkeeper two denarii. The cost for a night's lodging ranged from one thirty-second of a denarii for one-star accommodations up to one-twelfth of a denarii for a four-star establishment, which means the Samaritan covered between a month and two months of room and board. Then to top it off he also promised to reimburse the innkeeper for any additional expenses he might incur. Essentially, he wrote a blank check to do whatever was needed to care for this unknown Jewish man.

The parable of the Good Samaritan teaches us that instead of looking for the minimum amount to give to get by, a true Christian asks, "What is the maximum I can give and still take care of my other responsibilities?" You've probably seen a gift proposal that uses a "gift pyramid" to suggest the types of commitments needed to achieve a goal. The top of the pyramid might list one gift for $1 million, two gifts for $500,000, four gifts for $250,000, and so forth, all the way down to the entry-level gift of $1,000. This tool is effective because it shows where a donor might fit into a campaign. It's also an interesting exercise in human behavior to see how far down the pyramid your eyes drop before you're comfortable with an amount. Our minds might think "minimum," but our hearts should say "maximum."

5. Balance

An interesting part of the story is that the Samaritan left this man in the care of the innkeeper and continued on his journey. He had places to go, people to see, and things to do. The Samaritan was extremely generous, but he didn't stay with the person until he had fully recovered, nor did he give away all his money. He had other obligations. As a board member, you have several demands on your time and financial resources like family, church, your business, community, and the ministry in which you serve. It's important to give as much of your time and money as you can, while keeping your other obligations in balance.

Are You In?

It's easy to see where the Good Samaritan's heart was by looking at how he invested his time and treasure. Jesus used this story to convict the lawyer that he was looking for the easy way out instead of jumping in with total abandon. Margaret Thatcher once said, "No one would remember the Good Samaritan if he'd only had good intentions; he had money as well." If you serve on your board's nominating committee, start looking for candidates with more than good intentions. Recruit new board members who already have "skin in the game."

Jim DeVries—A Heart for Giving

Jim DeVries started his college career studying architecture, but after two years he changed his major and graduated from the University of Michigan with an engineering degree. While working in the medical field, Jim attained over one hundred patents in the areas of open heart surgery and cell separation equipment. In 1979, Jim founded DLP, a medical device company, which he sold to Medtronic in 1994. His company by that time had operations in three European countries and sold products to open heart surgery centers worldwide. God has blessed Jim with generosity. He's experienced the joy of helping ministries around the world, and he's also learned some valuable lessons about giving.

Jim, what has been the toughest lesson God has taught you about generous giving?

In 1995, the Lord led me to give a gift to help build a series of school buildings in India. I was closely connected with the mission and had complete confidence in them. However, three weeks after I gave the gift, the ministry lost the money in the Foundation for New Era Philanthropy debacle. New Era was a Ponzi scheme that operated from 1989 until its collapse in 1995 after having raised over $500 million from 1,100 donors. New Era convinced donors and ministries that their investments would be doubled in six months by a group of nine anonymous philanthropists. The scandal embezzled $135 million from individuals and charities, including more than 180 evangelical groups, colleges, and seminaries— including the gift I had just given.

I thought to myself, "I gave it to them and they lost it. It's their responsibility now." In my mind the matter was settled for a couple of days, but then the Holy Spirit began tugging at my heart. I got up in the middle of the night with the strong impression that the Lord was asking me to cover the loss with a second gift. He didn't let me rest until I took the check to the ministry a few days later. They were in disbelief. All I could say was, "Here, the Lord wants you to have this." Even though it was an incredible setback, the Lord taught me to trust him. I continue to hear news of how those Christian schools are making a difference in the lives of many children who in turn witness to their families. Over the years I've heard about many families that were revolutionized by their commitment to follow Jesus Christ! And in addition, a bit like a "Ponzi scheme," the tuition these non-Christian parents paid to send their children to these schools paid the expense of training a church planter who mentored these new Christians and planted many new churches. I'm glad the Lord pushed me to give the second time even though it didn't make sense. P.S. God saw to it that eventually most of the funds lost through New Era were returned to the organization as well!

How have you encouraged others to trust God for his provision?

A young man from our congregation felt called to serve an inner-city church on the East Coast. He asked me to help with a down payment on a home for his family, which I gave. A few weeks later, he called me again with the news that they had found the perfect house in the perfect location. The only problem was that it was a little more expensive than he could afford, so he asked if I could help with another gift. I said, "Are you sure this is the house God has for you?" He responded, "We are positive." To which I replied, "If you are certain this is God's plan, I want you to pray for the next forty days and ask God to provide the house for you." There was silence on the other end of the line, and then he countered, "But the offer expires in thirty days, and we will lose the house." I was firm. "You can pray about this, but don't talk to anybody about your need. Wait on God and see what he will do."

Forty days later, I got a phone call, and the first thing my friend said was, "You are never going to believe what happened!" I told him that I had a pretty good idea. The seller lowered his price, and the lender waived some closing costs, bringing the total to the point where my friend could afford to purchase the house. I could have given the additional gift, but I think it was more important for my friend to learn to trust God in a new way.

Some ministry leaders are uncomfortable about asking for a specific amount. How do you feel when someone asks you to consider a gift and they suggest an amount?

I am never offended when people suggest a gift amount. It lets me know what they have in mind. I might or might not give that amount, but I like knowing what they are thinking. Sometimes I give more than they ask. Recently, a development director shared a giving opportunity with me but never asked for money. That's fine, but in reality, she was looking for a gift. She could have just mailed a letter and saved us both some time. If she would have asked for $1,000, I would have written the check right then. But instead, she left a brochure, and I put it on my desk. The next week another ministry came and presented their need, then another, and then another. Her brochure quickly got buried in the bottom of my pile. The moral of the story is that it's okay to ask. I appreciate it when people ask for what they want.

Have you served on boards where some board members didn't give? How have you responded?

Everybody doesn't have to give the same amount, but everyone should give what for them is a generous, sacrificial gift. Often organizations seek funding from outside foundations. One measure they use to evaluate an organization is the percentage (not number) of board members who give to the organization. If it's less than 100 percent they might pass on giving a significant donation. If you don't believe in an organization enough to support it even modestly, please serve someplace else where you are passionate.

How would you encourage someone to excel in the grace of giving?

Not into this regularly giving thing? Start modestly. When Judy and I were married we were as poor as church mice! But God provided a great opportunity for me, and we began receiving a real paycheck. Decision time: pay off student debt or make a gift? We

> I am never offended when people suggest a gift amount. It lets me know what they have in mind.

chose to make modest contributions. The Lord seemed to honor that initial commitment and over the years has allowed us to continue to grow the absolute amount as well as the percentage we were able to give. If God has given you the gift of giving, you will become passionate about looking for new opportunities to give.

One additional note: I know the verse that says, "Do not let your left hand know what your right hand is doing" (Matt. 6:3). However, I don't think this applies within the family. It's important to involve your children early in a manner that's age-appropriate. At some point give them some additional money that they must give away. (No strings attached.) Later in life you will receive a blessing in return as they show they can be generous givers as well!

Action Step 2: Give

Group Discussion

1. **The financial commitment of our board can be characterized as:**
    - ❏ Stone Cold
    - ❏ Cool Ashes
    - ❏ Burning Embers
    - ❏ Raging Fire

2. **How can we encourage one another to give generously?**

    _____

    _____

3. **How important is it to our ministry that each board member gives? Explain your answer.**

    _____

    _____

4. **How should we communicate giving expectations to potential board members?**

    _____

    _____

5. **How can we appropriately communicate to our constituency the board's financial support of this ministry?**

    _____

    _____

Personal Reflection

What gift can I give that will stretch my faith?

ACTION STEP 3: NETWORK

Seek and You Will Find

In 1870, Russell H. Conwell sailed the Tigris River to Bag-dad, Nineveh, and Babylon. It was a marvelous trip, but his Arab guide was a non-stop storyteller who almost drove him crazy. Cromwell's only defense was to tune him out, but one day the guide told a story that captured Conwell's attention . . . and changed his life.

An ancient Persian named Ali Hafed owned a very large farm with orchards, fields, and gardens. He was a wealthy, con-tented man. One day a Buddhist priest visited him and shared the story of how diamonds were made. With just one diamond the size of his thumb, Ali Hafed could purchase a whole country. With a diamond mine, he could shower his children with great influence and wealth. Ali Hafed became discontent. Craving more, he asked, "Where can I find diamonds?" The priest told him, "Search for a river that runs over white sand between high mountains. In those sands are diamonds. All you have to do is go find them."

Ali Hafed sold his farm and left his family to search for diamonds. He wandered through the desert, through Palestine, and into Europe. He spent his fortune chasing a dream and ended his journey thousands of miles from home and completely destitute. He never found his treasure, and in despair, he took his own life.

One morning, the man who purchased Ali Hafed's farm led his camel into the garden to drink from the clear water in the brook. He noticed a flash of light and pulled out a black stone. Thinking nothing of it, he took it home and placed the stone on his mantel.

A few days later the old priest who had told Ali Hafed about diamonds came to visit the new owner. He saw the rock on the mantel and shouted, "Here is a diamond—here is a diamond! Has Ali Hafed returned?" "No, he has not returned and that is not a diamond; that is nothing but a stone; we found it right out here in our garden." But the priest said, "I know a diamond when I see it. I know positively that is a diamond." They rushed to the brook, sifted through the white sands, and found more diamonds more valuable than the first.

Ali Hafed's farm became the diamond mines of Golconda, the most magnificent diamond mines in history, which produced the great Kohinoor diamond in England's crown jewels and the largest known crown diamond on earth in Russia's crown jewels. Had Ali Hafed remained at home and dug in his own garden, he would have discovered "acres of diamonds."

Russell Conwell took this story back to America, and it became the foundation for his famous speech, "Acres of Diamonds," that he delivered more than six thousand times around the world. The jewel of Conwell's speech is that one need not look elsewhere for opportunity or resources; instead you should "dig in your own backyard!"

Chasing Mega Donors

What does this tale have to do with fundraising? Some organizations look far and wide for mega donors who can solve all their organization's financial problems. They dream about the Christian businessman in another town, another state, or even across the country and think, "If we could only meet that donor, they could give our lead gift."

If a donor's heart isn't aligned with your mission, their checkbook won't be either.

Occasionally, a well-meaning person will give a sage piece of fundraising advice and say something like, "I think you ought to go after Christian athletes; they have lots of money." But when you dig deeper and ask, "Do you know any Christian athlete personally, or know someone who does?" the response is usually, "No, but there are ways to find out who does." These folks, though good intentioned, are chasing dream donors.

That type of donor research is more detrimental than helpful because it focuses on a nebulous, unknown donor you might never uncover. Instead of chasing dream donors, you should "dig in your own backyard." Donors give to people and organizations that have touched their life in some way. The principle of Matthew 6:21 applies to fundraising: "For where your treasure is, there your heart will be also." When you capture a donor's heart, his financial investment will follow. But if a donor's heart isn't aligned with your mission, their checkbook won't be either.

Digging into Your Donor File

Chances are that the largest donor your organization will ever have is already in your donor file or is a close friend of someone in your donor file. Campaigns should have an emphasis on finding brand new donors, but the first strategy should be to identify and engage those people who already know and love your ministry. So take a closer look at your donors. Rank your donors' lifetime giving from top to bottom. Who has been giving consistently for years? Note any unusual gifts that stand out. Look beyond dollars and take note of people who always volunteer and attend events. What special relationship does that donor have with your board members, other key donors, or staff?

Add some external data to your internal knowledge about donors. Services like WealthEngine™, WealthPoint™, and Blackbaud's Target Analytics™ provide wealth screening that overlays your donor list with public sources of information to find wealth indicators. These scans identify income-producing asset holders, professionals with Keogh retirement plans, luxury property owners, SEC inside traders, business executives, professionals, foundation trustees, philanthropists, political donors, and those listed in Who's Who. A wealth screening will typically match 5 percent of your donors to a database that indicates they have some capacity to make a significant gift to your ministry.

The hard data of a wealth screening only tells a partial story. Take advantage of the soft data your human intel can provide. Friends, neighbors, church members, old classmates, and relatives can give you the inside scoop on a prospective donor. What are their giving interests? What other organizations and causes do they support? How is their business doing? Is now a good time to approach them? What would be a reasonable ask? As you get closer to a major donor, they might surprise you with the personal information they share about their giving, which might give you an indication of their interest and capacity to support your ministry.

A Diamond in the Rough

Jack was a long-time supporter of Grace Ministry. He had given systematically and occasionally stepped up for a $25,000 gift to help end their fiscal year in the black. Grace was ready to launch a capital campaign and conducted a Pre-Campaign Study to test their donors' potential buy-in. I met Jack in a coffee shop, and we chatted about how he was connected to Grace Ministry. When he went to the counter for some creamer, I looked out the window and thought to myself, "This guy is not a strong prospect." When he came back, we talked through my questionnaire, and I popped the question: "If Grace launches this campaign, would you support it?" "Yes, I think I will." "That's wonderful," I said. "Thank you very much! Could you estimate what your gift could be over three years?" He responded, "I've been thinking about this for a while, and now that I see they are serious, I think I could give $1 million." I almost fell off my chair. So much for my fundraising "Spidey sense!"

4.74 Degrees of Separation

In 1990, John Guare wrote a play titled *Six Degrees of Separation*. His idea builds on the "small world phenomenon" that everyone is approximately six or fewer steps away, by way of introduction, from any other person in the world. So, theoretically you could meet anyone on the planet through a chain of six friends or less. A funny twist on this concept is the game Six Degrees of Kevin Bacon, in which movie buffs attempt to link a random actor to Bacon through films the two starred in. Google has even created a "Bacon Number" for their search engine. Not to be outdone, Kevin Bacon got into the act by creating a website, SixDegrees.org, to encourage charitable social networks and inspire online giving.

We can see the phenomenon of social networking through the explosion of applications like Facebook, Twitter, and LinkedIn. Social networking is shrinking our world. In 2011, Facebook researched 721 million active Facebook users and their sixty-nine billion connections and discovered that only 4.74 people separate strangers from one another. One Facebook data team member blogged, "When considering even the most distant Facebook user in the Siberian tundra or the Peruvian rainforest, a friend of your friend probably knows a friend of their friend."[6]

> "Every one of our board members should constantly be in conversations with people to find out where God is hiding money!"

A Great Networker

Randy is a wealth manager who serves as the major-donor committee chair of a capital campaign. Often financial planners don't make great committee members for two reasons: (a) If they don't have a kingdom focus, they usually aren't interested in encouraging their clients to give away the money they manage, and (b) legitimately, they must guard their clients' confidentiality. Randy is the exception to the rule because he's kingdom focused. He passionately believes in the ministry on whose board he serves, and he also believes that if others know how the ministry is making an impact, they will give.

Randy wrote down a list of eighty-nine potential donors. Some were close friends he could call personally. Others were former clients or just individuals he knew with the capacity to give. In these cases he couldn't open the door, but his list was still helpful because he identified prospective donors other board members or staff might have overlooked.

"Namestorming" is a valuable exercise. Sit down and start listing all your potential contacts. Whom do you know from your past? Are any of your classmates someone who has lived up to their yearbook label, "Most Likely to Succeed"? Whom do you know from church? What business connections do you have? Is there anyone in your family who would be interested in getting involved? What about contacts at Rotary, Lions, Kiwanis, or the community prayer breakfast? As you think through your list, you'll begin to connect the dots. Maybe Aunt Mabel can't give, but what if she used to be the executive assistant to a local entrepreneur? "Namestorming" is like playing a real-life game of "Where's Waldo?" but with one caveat: Most major donors don't wear red-and-white-striped shirts with blue pants.

One board member expressed it this way: "Every one of our board members should constantly be in conversations with people to find out where God is hiding money!" Board members should develop a rolling top 10 list of prospects that pops up on their computer screen every morning. Then throughout the day as they interact with business associates, clients, and friends, they can think about ways to connect them to their ministry. This shouldn't be a static list but a living list that moves people from suspects to prospects, and prospects to donors, and then starts all over again.

Wayne and Betty served on a major gifts committee and attended a "namestorming" session to identify all the prospective donors in their circle of friends. Wayne said, "Back in 1927, I used to ride around in the milk truck with Dick, making home deliveries." Out of curiosity I asked, "Have you talked with Dick since then?" He replied, "Oh sure, we see Dick and Judy in the country club dining room every Sunday." Dick was on the ministry's radar screen because he owned a string of convenience stores, but we never had an open door to contact him. Even more frustrating, we couldn't get past Dick's executive assistant, who was an impenetrable gatekeeper. I asked Wayne, "Do you have his cell phone number?" "Sure!" I couldn't believe it and continued, "If you gave him a call, would he talk to you?" "Of course!" Behold the power of networking!

You might be 4.74 relationships away from a famous and wealthy Facebook friend who could be a major donor, but start with your cell phone contact list. Remember, the million-dollar donor in the coffee shop? No one dreamed that he had that kind of capacity.

Are you still reading this chapter? Go dig for diamonds!

Mike Richards—Banking on Friendships

On January 17, 1949, at the age of eleven, Mike Richards' life changed forever. On that day a nameless, faceless refinery worker gave his dad a pocket-sized Gideon Bible. As a result, the gospel completely transformed his dad. "So is my word that goes out from my mouth: It will not return to me empty, but will accomplish what I desire" (Isaiah 55:11). A friend also prompted Mike's dad, "You need to get those two kids in church." So Mike's parents took Mike and his sister to church, where they met Jesus. Mike still has that little New Testament to remind him how God's Word changed his life, and he has dedicated his life to being a nameless, faceless donor who gives so other people around the world can be transformed by the gospel.

Mike is a valuable board member because of his passion for God's Word and the impact it has had on his life. When people meet him, they immediately think of Biblica (formerly the International Bible Society). In fact, Mike is so vested in Bible translation and distribution that he's earned the title, "Mr. IBS." He understands the value of networking and has encouraged many of his friends to give to Biblica.

Mike, why have you been so successful in inviting new donors to give?

One reason for my effectiveness is simply that I've lived and worked in my community for more than fifty years. When you've been around that long you get to know a lot of people. But the real reason people give generously to Biblica is because its mission is so compelling. The eternal return on the investment is phenomenal. One major gift can impact an entire people group by making it possible to give them God's Word in their own native tongue. To be an effective fundraiser, you have to believe passionately in what your ministry accomplishes.

How has your business experience made you a better board member?

When I served as chairman of several banks, each board member had one of two purposes for being on that board: (a) bring all their business to the bank, or (b) network with their friends to bring more business to the bank. The overriding board objective was to drive bank deposits. Every board member, not just the officers, served on the business development committee and was expected to find new business. If they weren't willing to do that, there was no reason for them to serve on the board. We would host luncheons, tell business executives how our bank could serve them, and introduce friends to our leadership team. When you believe in something, it's easier for others to join you. Fundraising is exactly the same.

Describe the ideal board member.

Board members must, of necessity, be committed to that cause. Passion is the key. That's where the energy comes from. A board member's job is to give generously and then encourage others to join him in giving. I believe that board members must give their time, skills, and financial resources. Too many board members don't fully realize their fundraising responsibilities. A board member must understand that when you vote on a budget, you are also committing to doing everything in your power to achieve that goal.

Many boards have instituted Carver's Policy Governance model[7] to define the roles between the board and the CEO. As a result, some boards have delegated all fundraising responsibilities to the staff. How do you respond to this approach?

In every nonprofit organization, the CEO should be the number one fundraiser. That's because a business CEO wants to talk peer-to-peer with a ministry CEO. A major donor wants to look an executive in the eye and ask, "Can this person lead? Will they accomplish what they say they are going to accomplish? Do I trust them with my money? Do I like them?" Ministry leaders must be active fundraisers, but it's too big of a job for them to tackle all by themselves. That's where board members play an important role. We can bring our business networks to the ministry. We are out in the public arena everyday interacting with other executives and community leaders. Some of our associates are great prospects with values and giving interests that perfectly match our ministry's mission and vision. I can make those connections. At times I might hand the relationship over to our ministry leader to follow up; at other times I might stay the primary link between our ministry and that donor. It's not an either/or strategy; it's a team effort. Board members who take a hands-off approach to fundraising put their ministry at risk.

> A board member's job is to give generously and then encourage others to join him in giving.

If you could speak to a ministry board, how would you challenge them?

Well, they would probably only invite me once because I would ask some direct questions. (1) "What attracted you to this board?" (2) "Why did you accept your board position?" (3) "What do you specifically bring to the table that makes this a better board?" (4) "How are you advancing the kingdom of God by sitting on this board?"

I recently talked with a founder of a ministry that had twelve board members. He was frustrated because only one board member was giving. The founder had turned the board recruitment process over to a new executive director, and that person's only concern was recruiting board members from diverse professional disciplines like accounting, or auditing, or law, etc. A potential board member's financial capacity and commitment to giving was never even considered. Your giving reveals your passions, and by not giving you show that this ministry is not a priority with you. Matthew 6:21 states it clearly, "For where your treasure is, there your heart will be also."

What's been the most effective method you've used to introduce a friend to your ministry?

We've hosted banquets and small donor gatherings. These are helpful events to tell the ministry's story. My current strategy is to simply meet a prospective donor for lunch, or in their home or office, and share why I give and ask them to join me. Many of these people are my lifelong friends, who give to many projects. They are willing to take my phone call and appreciate direct conversations. I've learned not to beat around the bush but to be clear about what I am asking them to consider.

Share an experience when you encouraged someone to give generously and they gave beyond your expectations.

A few years ago we had a project to publish illustrated Bible materials for children. The project cost $1 million, and I decided to approach a friend for $500,000. I almost talked myself out of asking for the gift by thinking, "There's no way he'll give that amount." But I went and asked, and sure enough, he gave it. Since that time, over six million booklets have been printed in more than ten languages for children around the world. That person made an incredible gift, and that gift continues to make a global impact as those materials are being translated into more languages. People give generously when they understand what a project will accomplish for eternity.

Action Step 3: Network

Group Discussion

1. **The networking efforts of our board members can be characterized as:**
   - ❏ Stone Cold
   - ❏ Cool Ashes
   - ❏ Burning Embers
   - ❏ Raging Fire

2. **How can we hold one another accountable for networking?**
   _____
   _____

3. **How can we encourage every person in our ministry to network?**
   _____
   _____

4. **Should we conduct a wealth asset scan to help identify potential donors? If so, why?**
   _____
   _____

5. **As a group, "namestorm" one hundred prospects.**
   _____
   _____

Personal Reflection

Who are my top prospects whom I will introduce to this ministry?

ACTION STEP 4: INVITE

Build Your Donor Base One Friend at a Time

Rube Goldberg was a genius who devised incredibly complex solutions for simple tasks. His inventions were a series of chain reactions usually to be built with everyday parts like pulleys, ropes, gears, boots, bouncing balls, bows and arrows, springs, oscillating fans, and live animals. These contraptions had practical names: "Tooth Paste Squeezer," "Postage on Envelopes," "Way to Add Hair to Head," "Putting Cat Out at Night," and maybe one that has fundraising implications, "Loosen Up a Tightwad."

His comic strips included humorous instructions to describe his inventions. For example, in "No More Over Sleeping," he writes, "When sun comes up, magnifying glass (A) burns hole in paper bag (B), dropping water into ladle (C) and lifting gate (D), which allows heavy ball (E) to roll down chute (F), rope (G) lifts bed (H) into vertical position and drops you into your shoes (I)."[8]

Rube never intended to actually build the machines he drew, but his cartoons continue to inspire high school and college students. Each year aspiring young inventors compete to bring his imagination to life. Rube Goldberg machines and their creators often appear on late-night television shows and instantly become YouTube hits.

But what can Rube Goldberg teach us about fundraising? Some people think of fundraising as an elaborate machine with all sorts of moving parts, so they spend their time mapping out steps to move donors from "Glad to meet you" to "Would you please give us $1,000,000?" They believe that you can toss your donor base into the hopper and the machine will shake out dollars. Here are some strategies that can quickly become fundraising contraptions.

Designing the Perfect Brochure

Your organization needs at least two printed fundraising pieces, (a) a general brochure that explains your mission and impact, and (b) a case statement or gift proposal that outlines your need and solicits a gift. The general brochure is for everyone, and the gift proposal is a tool you share in a personal visit with donors. Brochures are effective tools to tell your story, but designing a "perfect" brochure is a trap. You can wordsmith your document to death with revision after revision. Aim for the best possible document, but don't let the process become so mired down in edits that you miss deadlines.

Brochure paralysis is annoying when you are trying to print a general informational brochure, but it is a fatal error when you need a personal solicitation piece immediately for a donor visit. Many major donors aren't impressed by the $5 brochure you created to ask them for a gift. Some will even question why you spent so much money. Many are entrepreneurs who scribbled out their business plan on a napkin over lunch. Don't fixate on creating a masterpiece.

Sometimes we can fall into the trap of believing that a fancy

Since 80 percent of your gift income will come from 20 percent of your donors, focus 80 percent of your time on engaging your top donors face-to-face.

brochure raises money. On a recent project, I helped an organization create a gift proposal. The photographs we chose were perfect, the copy was compelling, our charts were clear, and the ask was straightforward. The very first donor visit yielded a $250,000 gift. When I asked the ministry leader how he used the gift proposal in the conversation, he said, "Oh, I gave it to them after they said 'yes.'" These donors were long-time friends, and he realized that his relationship was more important than a piece of paper.

Liking Social Fundraising

No doubt, a well-meaning person has already suggested that your ministry must dive into social media fundraising. Every non-profit organization needs an up-to-date website to tell its story. But what about search engine optimization, the ability to make a donation online, e-blasts, texting donations, blogging, vlogging, offering an RSS feed, mobile apps, and of course, Facebook, LinkedIn, and Twitter? Technology is wonderful, but technology can also be a trap. You must evaluate each opportunity carefully to avoid investing dollars and time in strategies that might be cool but are not effective fundraising tools.

The internet is full of anecdotal stories of successful fundraising efforts driven by social media, but the real problem with social fundraising is converting a one-time donor into a long-term donor. Donors who give online but never receive any personal communication from that non-profit probably won't give again and certainly won't give larger gifts. Social media is a great tool for raising awareness about your organization and for receiving small gifts. Evaluate each social fundraising idea through the 80/20 grid. Since 80 percent of your gift income will come from 20 percent of your donors, focus 80 percent of your time on engaging your top donors face-to-face.

Chasing the Foundation Rainbow

One complicated solution ministries often consider is establishing their own charitable foundation. Many colleges, universities, and larger non-profits believe that donors are more inclined to give to a foundation than give directly to their organization. Because a foundation is a separate 501(c)(3) organization, donors might have more confidence that independent foundation board members will not be tempted to misuse endowment funds to bail out the organization. If your main reason for establishing a foundation is to add another layer of accountability, your organization might have a bigger credibility problem than a foundation can solve.

Foundation directors can become expert coaches for donors who want to leave a faith legacy for their family and need help navigating through complicated estate planning options. Many foundations manage the charitable trusts in their care. A foundation can become an effective fundraising arm for your organization. Ministry board members spend time deep into the weeds of programs, personnel, and strategic vision, but foundation board members have the freedom to focus on promoting the ministry to its constituency and the community. You shouldn't look for foundation board members whose primary responsibility is managing the money you already have. Recruit foundation board members who will help you find more money.

A foundation is another tool in your fundraising toolbox, but it costs time and money to create and maintain. A non-profit organization can promote planned giving without having a foundation. Donors do not automatically give just because you use the word *foundation*. In reality a foundation is just an empty bucket. You still need to tell your story, cultivate relationships, and ask donors to be generous. Before you build a foundation machine, consider the advantages and disadvantages. There is no magic pot of gold at the end of the foundation rainbow.

Skydiving for Jesus

In the "I-thought-I'd-heard-everything" category, on November 28, 2012, Pastor Rob Joy and a couple of friends jumped out of a plane to help raise funds for a new building for a brand new church plant in Wellingborough, Northamptonshire, about two hours north of London. I'm sure it was a blast and got a lot of press, but it probably wasn't a big moneymaker. Harvard University is launching a $6 billion plus campaign that will likely be the biggest university capital campaign in history. Don't expect to see their president jump out of a plane anytime soon.

This fundraising strategy sounds a little like *The Gospel Blimp*, a book and movie from the 1960s. Joseph Bayly wrote this satire to poke fun at Christian ministries that built elaborate systems but neglected the real work of evangelism. The plot focuses on George and Ethel, a friendly Christian couple who were concerned about their next-door neighbors but didn't know how to share the good news of Jesus Christ. One night during a gathering at their home with some Christian friends, a blimp flew overhead. Their friend Herm came up with a brilliant idea: Why not use a blimp to proclaim the Christian message to the unchurched citizens of Middletown? Herm's vision spawned a new non-profit organization with an exciting new strategy to buy a used blimp, hire a pilot, and evangelize their hometown by towing Bible-verse banners, broadcasting Christian music and programs over loudspeakers, and "carpet bombing" folks with gospel tracts. It's a great farce, if only it didn't hit so close to home. We will do anything in the name of evangelism—except talk to people about Christ. This same attitude infects fundraising.

Some systems-focused ministry leaders try to build the perfect fundraising machine with fancy brochures, social media, a foundation, or even a crazy event. Unfortunately, all these moving parts don't necessarily raise more money. Consider the opportunity costs of spending time on the wrong strategies. What can Rube Goldberg teach us about fundraising? One simple lesson: Don't build a fundraising machine. Build relationships.

A Simple but Effective Event

If you're not up for skydiving, or don't know where you can buy a blimp, why not just try introducing your friends to the ministry you serve? When Andrew heard about Christ, the first thing he did was to go tell his brother Peter (see John 1:41). There's nothing as powerful as a personal referral. Whether you're looking for a great restaurant, shopping for a new car, or researching a potential investment, your friends' opinions influence your decisions. You might have no problem telling a friend about your favorite plumber, but when it comes to asking them for money, you develop an acute case of laryngitis. That's unfortunate, because your friend might be interested in supporting your ministry—especially if they know that you are involved. A donor briefing is one friend-raising event that doesn't require a parachute. Here is what you need to know to get started.

1. What is the purpose of a donor briefing?

People give to people and organizations they know and love. A donor briefing is an intimate, warm gathering in your home, where you can introduce your friends to the executive director of your ministry and let him or her share their vision for ministry. The best fundraising strategy of all time is to simply tell stories of how the Lord is using your ministry to reach people for Christ. You can also share details about your strategic plan and how much money it will cost to turn your dreams into reality.

> Don't build a fundraising machine. Build relationships.

2. Do you take an offering or ask for money that evening?

No. This is not a fundraising event; it's a friend-raising event. The purpose of this gathering is to meet with potential donors and get a sense of their possible interest in your ministry. You shouldn't ask for a gift then for two reasons: (a) it might be uncomfortable to use your home for solicitation, and (b) the bigger reason is that people will not come prepared to give. Someone who might consider a $10,000 gift probably won't give it the very first time they hear your story. At the end of the presentation, you should hand out a response card and ask for the opportunity to visit personally with those who are interested.

3. What are the expectations for a host?

The host has five responsibilities:

    a.   Invite your friends with a letter and follow-up phone call.

b. Prepare light refreshments for the gathering.
c. At the beginning of the meeting, share briefly why you are involved.
d. After the meeting, send a thank you note to those who attended.
e. If you are comfortable with the next step, you could join your executive director for the follow-up visit with your friend(s).

4. Where should you hold this event?

Successful donor briefings can be held in many different locations like restaurants, hotel meeting rooms, country clubs, church fellowship halls, your ministry's board room, and even backyards. The best location is an informal, relaxed setting where friends can meet new friends. The most welcoming atmosphere is in your home.

5. Whom should you invite?

Invite people who have a heart for ministry and the capacity to give a significant gift if the Lord would lead them to get involved. Think of key leaders in your church, business associates, family, and friends.

A donor briefing only takes thirty days to organize. Start with an invitation letter, and then follow up with a phone call. Your letter should express why you love the ministry you serve and how you are involved. Here are some sample sentences:

Lisa and I are inviting a few friends to our home to meet Dr. Robert Williams, Executive Director of ABC Ministries. We would love for you to join us. Bob will be sharing how the Lord is using ABC to reach the next generation for Christ. He will also share the details of ABC's plan to remodel the chapel. We will not be taking an offering that evening, but Bob will be available to make appointments to personally visit those who would like to talk further about supporting ABC Ministries.

The ideal number depends on how many individuals you can comfortably fit into your living room. Most homes can accommodate a group of twenty to twenty-five. Remember, it's not how many are in the room but who is in the room that counts. Send an invitation to twice as many people as you hope will come.

6. What should be the schedule for the evening?

This is not an elaborate event but a small gathering with a relaxed agenda. The evening could look something like this:

6:30	Coffee
7:00	Presentation
7:45	Q & A
8:00	Dessert
8:30	Dismiss

7. Should you prepare dinner?

Some hosts/hostesses are gourmet chefs who want to prepare a banquet with all the trimmings. While that is very gracious, it is not necessary and can be a distraction. A donor briefing is just a simple fellowship time with coffee and dessert. At the end of the evening, allow enough time to mingle with folks and schedule follow-up meetings. It is easier to have these conversations in groups of two or three as opposed to sitting around a formal dining room table with a tall floral arrangement blocking your view.

8. What happens after the event?

You should send a personal note or make a quick phone call to thank everyone who attended. If you invited friends who were not able to come, call them to share the blessings of the evening and invite them to a future event. Then you can pass the baton to the ministry representatives, who can follow up with these new ministry friends and begin cultivating long-term relationships.

A Remarkable Story

The results of a donor briefing can be truly amazing. A few years ago a board member hosted an event in his home to introduce a few friends to the local rescue mission. The mission had launched a capital campaign to remodel an apartment building for their women's transitional housing program. Only four couples came, but remember, it's not how many come but who comes.

The board member welcomed everyone and shared a little about his and his wife's personal involvement with the mission. He introduced the executive director, who gave a brief summary of the mission's history, vision, programs, and impact. Then the director introduced the women's shelter director, who began her presentation with this stunning statement: "I spent seventeen and a half years behind bars." Instantly, she had everyone's attention. She went on to share her conversion experience and how God had totally changed her life.

This donor briefing would have been successful had it stopped right then—but wait, there's more! The women's shelter director had brought along a client who was graduating from the program. She was a beautiful twenty-three-year-old woman who had made some bad choices in life. Drug addiction landed her in jail, and she lost custody of her two young children. Upon her release from prison, she enrolled in the mission's transitional shelter program, where Jesus Christ miraculously transformed her life. She regained custody of her children and was starting over. Her fiancé attended the event with her, and they both reflected the joy that can only be found in Christ.

At the end of her testimony, there was not a dry eye in the room. The executive director closed the program and asked guests to fill out a response card, indicating when they might be available for a follow-up conversation. The hostess offered coffee and dessert, and everyone enjoyed a time of fellowship. Immediately, two couples asked if they could tour the facilities, and the director scheduled appointments right then.

One older couple made an interesting comment: "You know, the symphony visits us often and asks for $25,000 for this project and $25,000 for that project, but they aren't changing lives like this program." This gentleman was on the rescue mission's radar screen, but the executive director had never had a path to meet him. That night he became a friend of the ministry because a friend of his invited him to this event.

There is no magic formula for building a donor base. The best strategy is word of mouth as friends share with friends. The rescue mission connected with four new friends at this briefing without using a PowerPoint presentation, DVD, or full-color brochure. They just simply shared a powerful story of how Jesus Christ was impacting lives through their ministry.

Don't build a complicated machine; just invite your friends to join your cause.

Arch Bonnema—At Home with Major Donors

Christian entrepreneur Arch Bonnema has a zeal for giving. When he and Sherry got married, they decided to give 35 percent of their income to the Lord's work. Everyone who walks into Arch's office can clearly see his passion for advancing the kingdom. Written in gold letters along the top border of his wall are two verses: Jesus' prayer from John 17:4, "I have brought you glory on earth by finishing the work you gave me to do," and "Religion that God our Father accepts as pure and faultless is this: to look after orphans and widows in their distress" (James 1:27). Arch says, "Every morning when I come into my office, I look up and remind myself that God has something for me to do today."

Arch, who influenced you to become a generous giver?

I was blessed with two godly grandfathers. One was a farmer in Southwest Minnesota who sold his farm at the age of fifty so he could self-fund his missionary work. He served the Lord until he died at age seventy-four. My other grandfather was a successful businessman who enjoyed giving to missions and Christian education. Grandpa felt that God had taught him how to be a good businessman, and he wanted to glorify God with his time, treasure, and talents. When ministries came to visit, they expected to see some big tycoon, but he lived in a modest home in a small town. He was just generous, and gave away an enormous amount of money.

How has generous giving stretched your faith?

In 1990, Sherry and I attended a mission conference in Atlanta. We were riding home on our motorcycle, talking to each other through our helmet intercoms, when I said, "You know, honey, I have to admit I've been kinda feeling lately that we ought to increase our commitment from 35 to 50 percent, and that I should also give 50 percent of my business hours to the Lord's work." I hardly got done saying that when she said, "God's been telling me that for months. I was just waiting for you to confirm it with me."

When you make a decision like that, in the back of your mind you're thinking, "Wow—God is gonna really bless us now." But it doesn't always work that way. If you give, God doesn't always give back right away. That's where the prosperity gospel is wrong. There were times when my wife and I endured some big hardships, but we kept on giving. It wasn't that my business dropped off, but I spent less time doing it. My income dropped, but my giving increased, percentage-wise. "No problem," we thought. "We'll just sell some of our stuff we don't need anyway." To make sure that we kept our promises to missions, we gave everything we had, including cashing in our retirement, and even selling our two-year-old Cadillac.

It wasn't until we had given away pretty much everything over a span of six years that, all of a sudden, everything just reversed. God started building my businesses faster than I ever could have imagined. Within two years, I had more money than I had ever had in my whole life.

What is your current giving focus?

I've been blessed to travel to ninety-three countries. I usually avoid the big cities and prefer wandering through rural areas where you can see how people live. I've witnessed poverty, oppression, and violence—and people with only a few possessions who love God with a joyful heart. That's where my heart was first touched by orphans and widows. I saw a different world than the one I lived in. My heart changed in two ways: First, my passion for ministry increased tremendously. I saw how easy it is to change lives compared to here in the United States. When you see how easy it is to make a difference, it makes you want to do more. Second, it really opened my eyes to what it means to be a good steward. It's not about just writing a check. It's about giving to the right place at the right time.

The Lord connected me to Bishop Dr. Thomas Muthee, a pastor in Nairobi, Kenya, who founded Word of Faith Church, a forty-thousand-member congregation that has a Bible college, a community college, and a children's home. Word of Faith has started more than four hundred churches in Kenya, Southern Sudan, Tanzania, and Rwanda. They have grown in every area of ministry and have become one of the fastest growing multicultural congregations in Kenya.

Nine out of ten pastors in non-Western countries have less than one hour of formal education. In Africa, most pastors have been preaching for ten years before their church sends them for Bible training. It is so difficult for pastors to spend the time and money traveling to the college, so Bishop Muthee had a vision to take the college to the pastors. Each week professors travel to a church and hold a weeklong seminar for two hundred area pastors, then move to other areas for the second and third weeks before going home for a week. They are training six hundred pastors per month and, so far, more than four thousand have received training.

What fundraising advice would you give a board member?

I would ask several important questions: Are you giving generously on a regular basis? How many of your friends have you taken for a tour of your ministry in the last month? Who have you introduced to your ministry's executive director? Are you challenging your friends to give? Staff members should be telling the ministry's story to donors, but it's much more effective when board members tell the story and ask for a gift. Board members who get involved in fundraising are a tremendous encouragement to the staff and even other board members. I believe that if a board member isn't willing to invest their time and money, they should step down and let someone else lead.

How do you invite others to give generously?

Over the years, Sherry and I have hosted several small donor gatherings for many different ministries. We used to hold these meetings in a restaurant or a hotel meeting room, but those places can be cold and impersonal. We built our last home with ministry in mind. It had 12,000 square feet but only three bedrooms, because we wanted to use all the space we could for entertaining. With our indoor and outdoor areas we could comfortably host two hundred people for an event. For smaller gatherings, the formal dining room had two round tables that could each seat ten. We held a donor event in our home every two weeks for five years.

Some ministry leaders think that the most important part of these events is their PowerPoint, but the real business happens before and after the presentation as people sit around and talk. Hosting donor events in a home creates a warm, inviting atmosphere where people can feel comfortable. On several occasions people were having such a great time, I almost had to turn off the lights to get them to leave! I love helping my friends catch the vision for generous giving. I think every board member should host a donor gathering in their home and invite their friends to come hear about their ministry.

> Board members who get involved in fundraising are a tremendous encouragement to the staff and even other board members.

Action Step 4: Invite

Group Discussion

1. **Our donor relationships can be characterized as:**
   - ❏ Stone Cold
   - ❏ Cool Ashes
   - ❏ Burning Embers
   - ❏ Raging Fire

2. **Is our ministry more concerned about building a machine or relationships with donors? Explain your answer.**

   _____
   _____
   _____

3. **How can we personalize our approach to donors?**

   _____
   _____
   _____

4. **What fundraising strategies should we stop? Why?**

   _____
   _____
   _____

5. **What prevents us from launching a donor briefing strategy?**

   _____
   _____
   _____

Personal Reflection

When can I host a donor gathering in my home?

ACTION STEP 5: ASK

Fundraising Is for the Birds

Fundraising gets a bad rap among some Christian leaders who are uncomfortable with asking for money. They cite George Müller and Hudson Taylor as examples of great Christian men who told their needs to no one but God. Some modify that approach and are willing to share "full information" with donors, "but no solicitation." Others go so far as to suggest that personal solicitation is an unbiblical method that Christian organizations have adopted from the world.

This is a serious discussion for ministry leaders. What are the biblical methods for raising funds, and what strategies cross the line? Paul writes: "Command those who are rich in this present world not to be arrogant nor to put their hope in wealth, which is so uncertain, but to put their hope in God, who richly provides us with everything for our enjoyment. Command them to do good, to be rich in good deeds, and to be generous and willing to share" (1 Tim. 6:17–18). What does this command look like in real life?

The story of God's provision for Elijah in 1 Kings 17 is a compelling example. The chapter opens with Israel facing a severe drought and subsequent famine. But God generously provided for Elijah in the Kerith Ravine, east of the Jordan. Elijah drank from the brook, and twice a day ravens brought him bread and meat.

Elijah's situation might be similar to the fundraising strategy of many Christian organizations. Gifts appear out of the blue, but no one really knows who sent them. Every day development staff open letters filled with pieces of bread and meat. Once in a while, the ravens drop a big chunk of bread in the form of an estate check. But like Elijah, some ministries are seeing their money brooks dry up.

Thankfully, God's provision is not restricted by the severity of the famine, nor is he limited to one method for meeting our needs. He instructed Elijah to go to a widow in Zarephath, whom he had commanded to give food to Elijah. God's ways are not our ways. If we were in the same position, we might think a better plan would be for God to send us to someone who had more resources. But Elijah didn't question God; he just obeyed.

When Elijah arrived at the village gate, he met a woman gathering sticks. In a customary greeting, he asked her for a drink of water. As she was going to get it, Elijah called out, "And bring me, please, a piece of bread" (v. 11). This doesn't seem like a big deal, but for this woman, who was gathering sticks to bake a last meal for herself and her son, Elijah's request was outrageous.

She protested. She barely had enough for her family, much less a stranger. Elijah responded with a bold request. He told her to go bake the last cake of bread as she had planned, but he told her to give it to him instead. He added a promise: If she would put God first, her flour and oil would never run out. It's counterintuitive—it's faith.

God had commanded this widow to supply food for Elijah, so why does it seem like she didn't get the message? For those who take the position that all one needs to do is pray and God will supply, it seems that in this account, the widow should have offered a meal to Elijah without being prompted. Instead, she expressed fear and the stark reality that she simply didn't have enough to share. Isn't that the tension we all face when considering giving a gift? "If I give to the Lord, will I have enough for myself?"

Elijah's request made the widow consider other options. Responding to Elijah, she said, "As surely as the LORD your God lives" (v. 12), not "my God." The act of asking set everything in motion. The widow had to trust that Elijah's God would meet her needs—if she put Elijah first. She stepped out in faith, and the Lord miraculously supplied her needs. This account teaches at least four positive benefits of proactively asking for a gift.

1. Asking tests a donor's priorities.

The widow had a simple plan for her resources: Gather a few sticks. Make a fire. Bake a little bread. Eat a last meal. Die. Elijah's request shook her up. She had to reprioritize how to manage her resources, as meager as they were. Elijah's asking radically tested her faith. She had to give first to receive God's blessing. Would she believe and let go of what she had or hoard it for herself and die?

Today's donors face the same challenge. Do I lay up treasures in heaven or do I keep them for my security on earth? How can I be sure God will open the windows of heaven and pour out his blessings? We want to give by sight and check our bank account balances first. God wants us to give by faith. When a development director asks for a gift, they give a donor something new to consider. Perhaps making a generous gift wasn't even on the donor's radar. A request for support gives a donor an opportunity to respond in faith with a generous gift.

2. Asking triggers God's blessing.

Who really benefited from Elijah's request? Elijah did; he received bread. But the big winners in this transaction were the widow and her son. Before this encounter, they were doomed to starvation; afterward, they had abundant flour and oil for as many cakes as they desired. She literally went from famine to feast in one act of faith. Who benefits when a donor gives to a ministry? The ministry does, because it has the resources to fulfill its mission. But the major beneficiary of the gift is the giver. Paul encouraged the Philippians with this principle: " Not that I desire your gifts; what I desire is that more be credited to your account" (4:17). As a ministry leader, when you get to heaven, donors will thank you for having asked them to be generous to your ministry. They might even ask why you didn't ask them for more.

> When a development director asks for a gift, they give a donor something new to consider.

3. Asking teaches the asker to trust God.

In today's fundraising environment, a development officer would have run an asset screening on the widow of Zarephath and relegated her to the direct-mail-only file. Fundraisers fall into the trap of rating donors based only on external indicators. What do they do for a living? Where do they live? What kind of car do they drive? Generosity is not necessarily connected to a person's net worth. In fact, some wealthy Christians are paupers when it comes to giving.

Perhaps fundraisers should learn from this passage and base major donor qualifications on internal characteristics and move to the top of their donor lists those who are "rich in faith" (James 2:5). People in dire straits are forced to rely on God. Ministries need these prayer warriors more than they need money. Instead of approaching small and midrange donors through impersonal methods, maybe we should treat them with greater honor and ask for a gift with a personal visit.

Jesus said the widow gave more with her two mites than all the gold of the Pharisees combined (see Luke 21:1–3). We typically interpret this passage to mean that she gave more as a percentage because she gave all she had—100 percent. But could it also mean that God, in a miraculous way, multiplied her gift exponentially greater than all the other gifts? Maybe instead of seeking only donors with great capacity, fundraisers should solicit donors with great faith.

4. Asking establishes long-term relationships.

One serious downside to direct mail and other impersonal forms of fundraising is that they maintain the distance between the asker and giver. Personal solicitation bridges that gap. It's a conversation between friends. For Christians, it's a family discussion. Some Christian leaders are afraid to ask for money for fear that it will strain relationships. But asking for a gift can begin relationships that will last for eternity.

Because of Elijah's asking and the widow's act of faith, Elijah, the widow, and her son enjoyed food every day until the famine subsided. Imagine their fellowship around the table as they rejoiced in God's amazing provision. Think of Elijah's spiritual impact on the widow's son as he listened to God's word every day for months. Christian leaders who avoid personal solicitation and neglect to cultivate deep relationships miss incredible ministry opportunities.

Great things might happen when you ask boldly for a gift. God uses the request to stretch both the asker's and donor's faith. When the donor responds generously, no matter how meager the gift might seem, God honors that step of faith and miraculously provides for the giver and the asker.

If engaging donors by asking is such a large part of God's economy, why are Christian leaders so hesitant to step out in faith? Elijah's experiences demonstrate that God meets our needs in many different ways. Praise the Lord for the ravens who deliver God's blessing. And praise the Lord for those who have the faith to ask boldly and for those who give generously when asked.

Asking Might Be Hazardous to Your Nose

You might not be convinced that asking for a gift can actually strengthen your friendships. Unfortunately, not every Christian has a sanctified checkbook and is willing to give abundantly. Charles Dickens captured human behavior when he described Scrooge as "a squeezing, wrenching, grasping, scraping, clutching, covetous, old sinner!" Many struggle with an ownership mentality and haven't yet experienced the joys of cheerful giving. Even Christians who do have a heart for giving might be offended if you ask for a specific amount. Asking is risky, but not as risky as not asking. Your ministry's future is at stake.

Mark is a Bible-professor-turned-major-gifts-officer for a Christian college that launched a $30 million capital campaign. Bill was Mark's number one prospect. Mark had known Bill and Mary for more than twenty years and had often stayed in their home. Bill owned a successful manufacturing company and had given more than $1.8 million to the college over his lifetime, so it seemed reasonable to ask Bill and Mary to consider a $1.5

million campaign gift. But in his new development role, Mark was a little nervous about asking for a gift, especially a gift of that size.

Mark scheduled the meeting and called me for a pep talk. He said, "Ron, I know this guy. He's a straight shooter and a little rough around the edges. I'm afraid that when I ask for $1.5 million, he's going to punch me in the nose." I reassured him, "Mark, he's not going to punch you in the nose. If he does, you can come punch me in the nose. In any case, it's just your nose. This is your big chance to take one for the team!"

> Praise the Lord for those who have the faith to ask boldly and for those who give generously when asked.

Mark mustered up his courage and went to see Bill and Mary. Bill loves to golf, so Mark spent an afternoon enduring a little friendly ribbing about his swing. That night after supper, Bill said, "Okay, Mark, let's talk about why you came." Mark used a gift proposal to explain how the campaign would impact people for Christ all around the world. He got to the last page and asked, "Bill and Mary, would you consider a three-year commitment of $1.5 million?" Bill said, "I don't like people asking me for a specific amount, but we'll pray about it."

The following week, the president of the college called to thank Bill for meeting with Mark and to answer a few questions. They had a great conversation, but Bill again expressed that he didn't like people asking him for a specific amount and that he and Mary were thinking about what they might do. Over the next twelve months Bill transferred $1.1 million worth of stock to the college . . . and he's not finished yet! Thankfully, Mark was willing to risk his nose and ask for a gift. As a result, Bill and Mary were blessed by giving, the college was blessed by receiving, and Mark was blessed by avoiding hours of reconstructive surgery.

Mark continues to play bad golf with Bill. He sent Bill some college gear as a thank you gift, and Bill's response was, "That's the most expensive sweatshirt I've ever bought." Bill and Mary are always asking Mark to bring his wife, Brenda, along when he comes to visit, because they like Mark, but they love Brenda! Their friendship is stronger than ever.

Some think that fundraising is for the birds, so they wait patiently for gifts to appear out of thin air. But Elijah and Mark show us that good things happen when you trust God and ask for a gift.

Dave McGinnis—Making the Big Ask

When it's time for your fundraising campaign to "put feet on the street," you want someone like Dave McGinnis leading your major gifts team. Over the years, Dave has asked several major donors for significant gifts. Dave owns a manufacturing company, which means that he is his company's number one salesman. Dave is passionate about what he does, and his enthusiasm is infectious. Some people equate fundraising with high-pressure sales and imagine that asking for a major gift is like forcing someone to sit through a time-share pitch, but that couldn't be further from the truth. Biblical fundraising is simply inviting people to support the Lord's work, not pressuring them through manipulative sales tactics.

Relationship selling works because the seller cultivates a friendship with a prospect. The best sales people are those who honestly listen to a customer's needs and are interested in more than just closing the deal. They approach their customer with low pressure, openness, and honesty. This style of salesmanship wins a customer's business by offering a solution to a problem. Relationship selling is exactly like relationship fundraising. That's why Dave is such a good fundraiser.

Dave, how did you begin your stewardship journey?

When I was a young child, my parents mortgaged our small farm so they could give toward remodeling our country church. Our banker was so impressed that he remarked, "If someone is willing to borrow money for a church, I'm going to have to visit and see why for myself." My parents' generosity made a lasting impression on me. Nothing truly belongs to us; everything belongs to God.

What is God teaching you about giving?

Many times I've been tempted to think that I have accumulated wealth simply because I've earned it. After all, I got my first job before I graduated from high school. I served in the military, worked my way through college, and have worked fifty plus hours a week my entire adult life. I never took a vacation for the first fifteen years of our marriage, and until only recently I never took more than a couple of weeks off at a time. From my human perspective, I want to take credit for my success, but then I remember that God is the giver of life and every good gift. He has blessed me with energy, great health, and a wonderful wife. I want to give back to him with a joyful heart.

Why have you served on capital campaigns?

I serve on a college board of directors, and our president asked me to consider chairing our capital campaign. I thought to myself, "There is no way I'm doing this!" but I agreed to pray. A couple of weeks later I took a sales trip and came down with a severe case of pneumonia. As I was lying in my hospital bed, all I could hear was God saying, "Give me one good reason why you can't lead this campaign." I couldn't come up with anything, so I volunteered.

"Just Do It!" Frankly, you might like it.

What's been the most enjoyable part of asking for a major gift?

I never once asked for a gift that upset someone. I surprised a few people, but no one ever got mad. It was a very pleasant experience. If you are upfront with people and tell them why you are coming, many times you leave the meeting with a check and a new friend. As chair, I solicited all the campaign leaders for their commitments. Interestingly, instead of straining our relationships, I found that these conversations often created special bonds. I remember one particular conversation with Jerry, a committee chair and fellow board member who took me into his confidence. He shared his heart for ministry and spoke openly about his giving priorities. We had worked together on the board, but from that day forward we shared a unique camaraderie. In my experience, asking for a gift actually strengthened my relationships with these friends.

Share one lesson you have learned from a major donor about asking for a gift.

The president and I made a call on an individual who lived across the street from our campus. This donor shared that his neighbor was thinking about selling his property and that it would be a perfect acquisition for the college. We visited the neighbor and learned that he was asking $150,000. The president thought we should go back to our first donor, give him an update, and ask him for the $150,000 we needed to buy his neighbor's house for the college. He gave it! It pays to listen to your donor's suggestions.

What's the funniest thing that's ever happened to you on a major donor call?

I visited a man in Florida who had been very generous. We were constructing a new building on campus, and I presented him with a naming opportunity. I said, "Harold, you've meant a lot to our college and to me personally. I'd like to see your name on that building so every time I visit campus I will think of you." Harold responded, "You know, Sonny, you don't put your name on buildings, because some other young whippersnapper like you will think you've got money and won't quit bothering you!" Harold gave the gift, but not his name.

How would you encourage a board member who doesn't have the "gift" of asking?

Board members have different abilities, just like church members have different spiritual gifts. Some people have the gift of giving, and some people don't, but those who don't still need to give. Some people have the gift of evangelism, and some people don't, but those who don't still need to share their faith. Asking for money is similar. Some board members are wired for sales, so asking for a gift comes naturally. Other board members might be more reserved, but that doesn't earn them a free pass to avoid fundraising. Board members must do everything in their power to promote their ministry. Everybody needs to ask somebody, but some are better askers than others.

What advice would you give someone who has never asked for a significant gift?

First of all, people like personal attention. Everybody has a story, and I love to hear their story. If you are interested in another person's story you are probably a good candidate for the major gifts committee. Ask yourself, "What's the worst thing that could happen?" Nobody has ever sworn at me or punched me! The best advice I can give sounds like the Nike commercial, "Just Do It!" Frankly, you might like it.

Action Step 5: Ask

Group Discussion

1. **Personal solicitation by our board members can be characterized as:**
   - ❏ Stone Cold
   - ❏ Cool Ashes
   - ❏ Burning Embers
   - ❏ Raging Fire

2. **As a board, do we view asking as ministry or a necessary evil? Explain your answer.**

   _____

   _____

3. **Do we approach fundraising as transactional or transformational? Why do you think so?**

   _____

   _____

4. **Does asking strengthen or weaken friendships? Why do you think so?**

   _____

   _____

5. **Share an experience when you asked for a gift.**

   _____

   _____

Personal Reflection

In the next thirty days, whom can I ask for a gift to support this ministry?

ACTION STEP 6: WORK

I'd Rather Be Digging Dirt with a Shovel

We started this conversation about fundraising by emphasizing the importance of prayer. Remember the second half of St. Augustine's proverb? "Work as though everything depended on you." Fundraising is hard work.

Maybe you don't verbalize your feelings in a board meeting, but your frustrations are real. You might be an energetic executive director or a dedicated board member, but you're discouraged because not many people in your ministry are trying to raise money. Even worse, maybe you're annoyed that some board members don't even give. If you feel this way, you are not alone. Askers always struggle to motivate non-askers to participate in fundraising. Before you write your resignation letter, consider these words from the apostle Paul:

"Get along among yourselves, each of you doing your part. Our counsel is that you warn the freeloaders to get a move on. Gently encourage the stragglers, and reach out for the exhausted, pulling them to their feet. Be patient with each person, attentive to individual needs. And be careful that when you get on each other's nerves you don't snap at each other. Look for the best in each other, and always do your best to bring it out." (1 Thess. 5:13–15, The Message)

Paul wasn't specifically writing to executive directors and board members, but if you apply his principles of working together to fundraising, you might actually look forward to monthly board meetings! You probably know this already, but each board member has different strengths and weaknesses. They see fundraising from different perspectives, so you must motivate them in ways that resonate with them. Paul suggests four approaches for working with people:

> Askers always struggle to motivate non-askers to participate in fundraising.

1. Warn the freeloaders to get a move on!

Effective fundraisers share two common denominators: skill and will. Most can learn the skills of fundraising, but if an executive director or a development director doesn't have the desire to raise money, they probably won't. They might make an effort for a while, but most people ultimately drift back into their comfort zones and avoid uncomfortable tasks.

In Jesus' parable of the two sons (see Matt. 21:28–31), one son immediately agreed to his father's request to work in the vineyard but never followed through. The other son initially refused to work in the vineyard but later repented and got to work. World-renowned violinist and music educator Shinichi Suzuki once said, "There is no merit in just thinking about doing something. The result is exactly the same as not thinking about it." You might believe that making personal donor calls is the right fundraising strategy. You might even agree that it's an important part of your job description. But until you schedule appointments with donors, go visit them face-to-face, and ask for a gift, your major-donor strategies are just good intentions.

Successful fundraising requires actions, not words. Quit waiting for the ideal major-donor call. Stop redesigning the perfect promotional brochure. Don't worry about exactly what you will say when you meet the donor. Put your fears and excuses behind you. Pick up the phone and make the call. Be the son who works in the vineyard.

2. Gently encourage the stragglers.

Some board members have trouble following through with fundraising responsibilities. People have a thousand things to do, and there aren't enough hours in the day to get it all done. Tasks like setting up a major-donor call tend to fall to the bottom of the to-do list. Come alongside your busy board members and encourage them to keep moving forward with your fundraising plan. Maybe all it will take is for you to sit down in their office and review their assignments. Your enthusiasm for fundraising can motivate others.

Unfortunately, some board members never complete their assignments. They keep promising to contact a potential donor, but they neglect to make the phone call. They talk a good game, but it's just talk. Solomon describes these board members, and even a few donors this way, "Like clouds and wind without rain is one who boasts of gifts never given" (Prov. 25:14). The Corinthian church was slow in sending a gift they had promised, so Paul wrote and challenged them to follow through and get the job done (see 2 Cor. 8:10–11). It's not what you *expect* but what you *inspect* that actually gets done. Encourage board members to take an active role in fundraising. If nothing changes, refer to step one.

3. Reach out for the exhausted.

Don was the rare board member who jumped into a capital campaign with both feet. He was a retired contractor who had built a strong donor prospect list that included business associates, community leaders, church members, and lifelong friends. As he made donor calls, he discovered that many of his contacts weren't as excited about the capital campaign as he was. Some didn't want to meet with him. Some wouldn't return his phone calls. Some put off a decision to give. Others gave considerably less than he had hoped.

At one board meeting he shared, "This is hard work. I'd rather be out digging dirt with a shovel than asking people for money." Don needed someone to come alongside and encourage him. He was doing a great job. Donors weren't eager to give because the organization had done a poor job of telling its story, not because Don was doing something wrong. With some encouragement, Don kept pitching. At the end of the campaign he had raised three times more than anyone else on the committee. Reach out to exhausted board members and pull them to their feet.

4. Be patient with each person.

The stress level at board meetings usually tracks with the monthly financial reports. As gift income rises, so does everyone's mood, but when donations go down, attitudes often follow. The executive director looks at the board and wonders why they aren't helping. The board looks at the executive director and wonders why he or she doesn't get out and call on major donors. Remember the verse we started with, "And be careful that when you get on each other's nerves you don't snap at each other. Look for the best in each other, and always do your best to bring it out" (1 Thess. 5:13–15, The Message).

What can an executive director do to bring out the best in board members? And what can board members do to bring out the best in an executive director? You need a plan and some patience. The plan is simple. Fundraising is all about relationships. It's not a great piece of mail or a new color brochure; it's sharing your story with donors one at a time. Look at your prospect list together and develop a personal strategy for each donor. Which board member knows this person the best? Who should go with the executive director to make a presentation? Is the purpose of this donor call to introduce the ministry, cultivate relationships, or ask for a gift? Who will follow up with the donor? Once you've done your homework, grab a board member and go make a donor call together. You'll be pleasantly surprised at what God can do.

Don was right. Fundraising is hard. Some of your board members might even rather "dig dirt with a shovel." But when you work together to bring out the best in every team member, the tough times get easier and the good times get even better.

A Cold Drink of Water

Their family couldn't believe they were moving to some godforsaken little town in South Dakota, but Ted and Dorothy had prayed about it and felt that God was leading them to buy a small drugstore there. Then after five long years of hard work, customers were still few and far between, and they began to wonder if they had made the right decision.

One hot July afternoon in 1936, Ted watched the store while Dorothy took the kids for a nap and to take one herself. She couldn't sleep because of all the noise from the traffic passing by on the way to Mount Rushmore, and then an idea popped into her head. Just three little words might entice those hot, thirsty travelers to stop: free ice water.

It was a stroke of genius. Dorothy wrote a little poem to welcome weary travelers, and Ted mounted it on several boards spaced apart like the old Burma Shave highway signs. "Get a soda . . . Get a root beer . . . Turn next corner . . . Just as near . . . To Highway 16 & 14. . . Free Ice Water. . . Wall Drug." The next weekend Ted put up the signs, and by the time he got back to the store it was jammed with people clamoring for free ice water.

They poured gallons of ice water for hours, made ice cream cones, gave highway directions, and sent travelers on their way refreshed and ready for adventure. Today, more than twenty thousand visitors stop in every day for a refreshing glass of free ice water.

Refreshing others is a biblical concept. Absalom rebelled against his father, King David, causing David and his household to flee for safety. As they were leaving Jerusalem, Ziba, Saul's former servant, showed up with some provisions for their trip and said to David, "The donkeys are for the king's household to ride on, the bread and fruit are for the men to eat, and the wine is to refresh those who become exhausted in the wilderness" (2 Sam. 16:2). Ziba was thinking ahead and knew that David and his entourage would quickly become exhausted. David was so grateful for Ziba's kindness that he blessed him with a great reward. Ziba refreshed David, and Ziba was refreshed in return.

> What would happen if you prayed for your top one hundred donors by name?

No one has to tell you that fundraising is exhausting—especially when you ask and ask and ask and keep coming up dry.

If your throat is parched from telling your story to people who aren't responding, be refreshed by three encouraging truths from Psalm 107.

> *Some of you wandered for years in the desert,*
> *   looking but not finding a good place to live,*
> *Half-starved and parched with thirst,*
> *   staggering and stumbling, on the brink of exhaustion.*
> *Then, in your desperate condition, you called out to GOD.*
> *   He got you out in the nick of time;*
> *He put your feet on a wonderful road*
> *   that took you straight to a good place to live.*
> *So thank GOD for his marvelous love,*
> *   for his miracle mercy to the children he loves.*
> *He poured great draughts of water down parched throats;*
> *   the starved and hungry got plenty to eat.*
> (Psalm 107:4–9, The Message)

Truth #1: Desperate times call for desperate measures.

We've already talked about how vital prayer is to your fundraising effort, but it's important to bring it up again in this chapter about hard work. Are you feeling desperate? The psalmist reminds us, "Then, in your desperate condition, you called out to GOD" (v. 6, MSG). You know from your personal walk with God that prayer is hard work. Why should it be any different in your organization's life? If we were brutally honest with ourselves, some of us would have to admit that praying about our financial needs is often just an afterthought.

Maybe God is leading your organization through a financial desert so you will quit trusting in your own abilities and place your faith in him. How would your ministry change if your board, your executive team, and your staff prayed and fasted for God to meet your financial challenges? The believers in Jerusalem were prompted to pray for those who had generously responded to their needs (see 2 Cor. 9:13–14). What would happen if you prayed for your top one hundred donors by name? There's only one way to find out.

Truth #2: God's timing is always perfect.

God has a master plan and allows us to face trials to teach us perseverance. Mountains test our faith and give God an opportunity to show his strength. The psalmist reminds us that God rescued the children of Israel "in the nick of time!" (v. 6). Scripture is filled with testimonies of God showing up at just the right moment to save the day. Moses and the children of Israel found themselves hemmed between Pharaoh and the deep Red Sea, but God provided a way out that no one could have imagined. Things got a little hot for Shadrach, Meshach, and Abednego when they stood up for God, but he showed up just when they needed him most. Peter stepped out of the boat in faith, but the storm distracted him and caused him to sink. In desperation he cried out, and the Lord saved him just in the nick of time!

Whatever your financial situation is, God can show up and solve your problem. He's brought your organization to this moment to teach you something about you and something about him. Maybe your financial stress will prompt you to manage your resources better. Maybe these tough times are designed to push you out of the office to go meet with donors. Maybe this moment will rally your board to step up and lead your fundraising effort by giving generously themselves and asking others to give. Perhaps your fundraising test will end like Job's. "But he knows the way that I take; when he has tested me, I will come forth as gold" (Job 23:10).

The whole point of Psalm 107 is to praise God for his miracles. "So thank God for his marvelous love, for his miracle mercy to the children he loves" (v. 8). We sometimes forget that God is still in the miracle business. That's no excuse for being lazy, but it's reassuring to know that after you have done all that you can do, God can do the rest. How big of a miracle do you need? Are you trying to avoid cutting staff? Does your building have deferred maintenance issues that you've put off too long already? Do you need a leadership gift to launch a capital campaign that will accomplish your vision? Cry out to God and he will "put your feet on a wonderful road" (v. 7).

Truth #3: Refreshing water comes from unusual places.

God answers prayer "immeasurably more than all we ask or imagine" (Eph. 3:20). The psalmist declared that "He poured great draughts of water down parched throats; the starved and hungry got plenty to eat" (v. 9). Sometimes God supplies through unusual sources. When Moses struck the rock, a river gushed out to satisfy their thirst (see Exod. 17).

Gary was a retired firefighter who lived in a two-bedroom basement apartment and had faithfully given $200 every month for more than ten years to Hope Ministry. Steve, the executive director, decided to visit Gary and share about Hope's capital campaign. As he sat in the living room, Steve assumed that Gary was probably already giving as much as he could, but he decided to ask for more anyway and let Gary decide for himself.

Steve explained how this campaign would help Hope Ministry reach more people and showed him a table of gifts. Then Steve and Gary had this incredible conversation:

> Steve: "Gary, would you consider a generous gift to our campaign?"
> Gary: "I think I'd like to give $500."

Steve: "Thank you so much. That's wonderful! Do you mean a one-time gift, or do you mean $500 per month?"

Gary: "$500 per month."

Steve: "Thank you very much. That's a wonderful gift. Now just to be clear, the campaign lasts for three years. Are you thinking about giving $500 each month for one year or for the entire campaign?"

Gary, matter-of-factly: "I can give $500 a month for three years."

Steve thanked Gary again and ended his visit. When Steve got to his car, he still couldn't believe what had just happened. Gary appeared to need financial help, but instead he made an incredible $18,000 commitment. Steve was even more amazed when he realized that Gary had just pledged more than most of his board members.

Solomon reminds us, "A generous person will prosper; whoever refreshes others will be refreshed" (Prov. 11:25). Gary understood the power of generosity and was ready to refresh Steve and his ministry. When you've been working hard all day in a fundraising desert, ask God to send you someone with a cup of cold water.

Kevin Knowlton—Working by the Non-Billable Hour

Lawyers, financial planners, and accountants are not necessarily effective fundraisers for two reasons: (a) they are extremely busy people, and (b) many are uneasy about soliciting prospective donors they might know professionally for fear it will hurt their business. Kevin Knowlton is an exception to the rule. He is a member of the board of trustees of a Christian college and serves as chairman of the board of a Christian school. Kevin is a senior partner in a leading law firm, but you might not realize it because of all the non-billable hours he invests in serving Christian ministries.

Some board members serve lots of organizations, but their board work seems to be limited to two hours per month. Kevin is the rare board member who serves only a few ministries, but with great depth. He throws his whole heart, soul, mind, and strength into promoting the ministry in every possible way. It's not unusual for Kevin to call a ministry leader late at night or early in the morning with a great idea that just came to mind. He is a tireless worker.

Kevin, you are extremely busy with work, family, and church responsibilities. How do you find the time to serve as a board member?

The key is intentionality. It's like anything else in life; you always make time for what's important. I never missed one of my kids' basketball or soccer games. I take serving as a board member just as seriously. As an attorney, I have more flexibility than physicians or dentists who see patients all day. I usually know in advance when I have a board or committee meeting, so I'll block off my calendar. There are always things that come up, but you have to learn to juggle your board responsibilities with everything else. Regular board meetings take time, but the real time commitment comes between board meetings, working on all the special committee assignments. I think board members who don't make their board membership a priority won't be very effective.

Do you see your board service as a calling from God?

Some people want to be on a board to network or build their resume, but I'm not looking for any prestige or recognition. I've served on secular non-profit boards in the past, but I no longer volunteer for organizations such as the arts council or the theatre because I believe that God has gifted me with certain skill sets to advance his kingdom. I want Christians to serve on community boards, but my passion is Christian education. I have no doubt that I am doing exactly what God has called me to do.

Why is serving on a board so satisfying for you?

I have a friend who serves on almost every non-profit board in the community because he wants to be salt and light in as many places as he can. He's making an incredible difference, but his involvement on some boards is limited simply because of time constraints. I've decided to serve just a few ministries and drill down deep. Christian organizations must strive for excellence to make the greatest impact they can. I'm never satisfied with mediocrity, so I want to give my best. It's incredibly satisfying to see how God uses the ministries I serve to change lives for eternity.

You always clear your schedule to help the development director when he calls. Why are you so passionate about serving?

I am willing to drop other things because serving on a ministry board is my priority. If that means I need to be flexible, I'm willing to do whatever it takes because I'm so passionate about our mission. I don't know if it's just my personality, or if it's something that can be learned, but I can't do anything half-heartedly. I've got to serve with everything I've got.

How does your professional expertise help you be a more effective board member?

Christian organizations today face new challenges they've never faced before. I have experience in many different areas: healthcare law, education, litigation, insurance, regulation, and construction, so I can bring a lot of knowledge to the board. Not everybody has to be like me. It's like the body of Christ; every person has a unique set of gifts they bring to the table, but if your board is all "eyes" or "ears" you might struggle to get things done. You need a few "feet" willing to get out and ask for money.

> Board members who don't make their board membership a priority won't be very effective.

Who influenced you to get involved in Christian leadership?

When I graduated from college, I had no idea that I would serve the Lord in this way. Blair Dowden was the Vice President for Advancement at Houghton College and later served as President of Huntington University. While at Houghton, he took an interest in me and invited me to join the President's Advisory Council. That experience was instrumental in fanning a passion in my heart for Christian education. I now serve on the Board of Trustees of Houghton College and chair the Board of Directors of Lakeland Christian School. Christian leaders need to look around and pour their lives into the next generation of leaders.

Some board members are reluctant to solicit their clients, partners, and business associates for fear it will adversely impact their business relationships. Why are you so bold?

When you agree to serve as a board member, you are lending your credibility and professional reputation to that organization. A board member's presence on a board should give other donors confidence that the organization is worthy of their support. Development directors are paid to ask people for money, but it makes a big difference when a volunteer asks. I've never hesitated in asking someone for support. Other people contact me all the time, and I'm never offended. To me, it's a privilege to talk with someone about a ministry I truly believe in.

If I were obnoxious about how I approached people that would be different. It doesn't work if you are pushy, demanding, and expecting. I don't make cold asks, but just present the need and trust God to work in that person's heart. You don't want to be that guy who was afraid to ask for a gift for fear of offending someone, and then find out later that the donor gave a big gift to another organization because they had the courage to ask. I enjoy meeting new people and developing new friendships. It's fun to see someone else catch a passion for your ministry. Instead of harming my business relationships, I've found the exact opposite to be true. My involvement in fundraising has strengthened my friendships, not weakened them.

Would you recommend working with a fundraising consultant?

Fundraising is hard work. It's not about sitting around and waiting for envelopes with money to come in the mail. For our Lakeland Christian School capital campaign we brought in Pat McLaughlin from The Timothy Group to coach us through the process. Our board, administrator, and development director had never raised that kind of money before, and we knew we needed help. Our board learned a lot from Pat's book, *Major Donor Game Plan*, because it was filled with so much practical advice. But the real difference Pat made in our campaign was getting out in the field and making donor calls with us. Showing us how to ask made all the difference. I highly recommend Pat and The Timothy Group to any Christian organization that wants to take their ministry to the next level.

Action Step 6: Work

Group Discussion

1. **The level of engagement by our board members can be characterized as:**
   - ❑ Stone Cold
   - ❑ Cool Ashes
   - ❑ Burning Embers
   - ❑ Raging Fire

2. **How can we encourage one another to strive for excellence?**
   _____
   _____

3. **Can we honestly share our discouragements with one another? If not, why not?**
   _____
   _____

4. **What specific board action can we take to encourage our development team?**
   _____
   _____

5. **How can we increase board involvement in fundraising?**
   _____
   _____

Personal Reflection

Am I serving this organization wholeheartedly?

ACTION STEP 7: THANK

How Can I Say Thanks?

A major donor looked the new executive director in the eyes, pointed his finger, and scolded, "Don't *ever* forget to thank your donors." Wow, that should get your attention. The donor had given a sizeable gift and, unfortunately, the former director had forgotten to say, "Thanks."

Forget your keys, forget your mother's birthday, even forget your anniversary, but never forget to thank your donors. Ten lepers were healed, but only one returned to thank Jesus for his wonderful gift (see Luke 17:11–19). Evidently, the other nine were too busy enjoying their new lives and didn't have time to show their appreciation. Not much has changed.

How well your organization shows appreciation to donors becomes an important factor in whether your donor cultivation cycle keeps moving forward or grinds to a halt. Maybe you've heard this fundraising proverb: "Thank the donor seven times before asking for another gift." Thankfulness can take many forms—a handwritten note, a small gift of appreciation, or a personal phone call from staff or board members.

In this age of annoying telemarketing calls during supper, many organizations have an aversion to contacting donors over the phone. However, a thank you call will set your organization apart from the rest. Calling a donor is not an annoyance. It's ministry. It's a friend calling a friend to say, "Thanks." Donors should never feel that their gifts are expected, taken for granted, overlooked, or unappreciated. The sole purpose of the thank you phone call is to make a personal connection with the donor and express your gratitude for how their gift has helped your organization. Here are five easy steps to make donor thank you calls.

> Donors should never feel that their gifts are expected, taken for granted, overlooked, or unappreciated.

1. Set Attainable Goals

Focus on your top 100 list. It helps to assign callers to contact donors they already know, but that's not necessary. Start at the top and work down. Top donors should be called by the executive director or board members. Set realistic goals and expectations. Some staff and board members will find this to be challenging, others will take to it naturally. Assign ten names to each caller and set a time when you would like to have the calls completed. Have additional names ready for those who complete their list quickly and are eager to contact more donors.

2. Script Callers

Make this job as easy as possible by creating a script for your volunteers to follow. Encourage your callers just to use the script as a guide. The real joy in these calls is having personal conversations with friends.

- *Good evening. My name is _____, and I'm a (board, staff) member of New Life Ministry.*
- *How are you tonight?*
- *I'm calling to thank you for your financial support for the ministry. We depend on the partnership of friends like you to make a difference and we appreciated your gift.*
- *The Lord is using New Life to accomplish some wonderful things in people's lives . . .*
- *How long have you been associated with New Life Ministry?*
- *Have you attended any ministry events recently?*
- *Do you have any prayer requests that you would like to share with our ministry family?*
- *It was good to talk with you. Thank you again for your prayers and support.*
- *Good night.*

A thank you call only needs to last ten to fifteen minutes, unless the donor wants to continue the conversation.

3. Leave a Message

The goal of thank you calls is to make a personal connection with your donors. Your donors lead busy lives, however, and might be difficult to catch. Try at least three times to have a personal conversation with the donor before leaving a message on their answering machine. But do leave a message rather than making no contact at all.

4. Listen Carefully

The purpose of this call is not to update donor records. However, in the course of your conversation you might learn helpful information the organization needs to have (change of address, a death or sickness in the family, etc.). Notify the development department of any database changes and any prayer requests that should be shared with the ministry family.

5. Offer Prayer

It's always appropriate to offer to pray for someone. It might be appropriate to pray for them during your phone call, especially if the donor shares a serious prayer request. Be sensitive to the prompting of the Holy Spirit in these situations. You might be a blessing to someone who needs encouragement.

One executive director took this attitude of gratitude to heart and called a foundation director to thank him for a $10,000 gift. The foundation director was very appreciative of the call and mentioned that organizations rarely thank them for grants. His comment launched a half-hour conversation. They talked about the ministry's impact, plans for growth, and financial needs.

The foundation director then made this incredible comment: "When we evaluate grant proposals, we determine the maximum amount we will award and then give the organization a portion of the grant. If the organization keeps the lines of communication open, we then consider giving more. If we never hear from them again, eventually we distribute those funds to another organization. Thanks for calling. I would like to increase our grant this year to $25,000." It pays to be thankful.

Donor Recognition

Walk into the lobby of most non-profit organizations and you will notice a beautiful wall display in a prominent location that acknowledges donors who have contributed to the annual fund, capital campaign, endowment, or some special project. Donor recognition systems have come a long way from the old school rectangular sign with bronze name tags. Today's systems are works of art that creatively thank donors for their generosity. Some ministries agonize over designing just the right display. What style should it be? Who all should be included—board members, campaign committee members, staff, and volunteers? Should donors be arranged by the amount they gave, or would our constituency rather see donors listed alphabetically? How should we acknowledge our lead donors appropriately?

Deciding how to publicly show your appreciation to donors is an important discussion, but another aspect of donor recognition is even more important. What if we reversed this topic and defined donor recognition as how well a donor can recognize you? If your executive staff and board members stood in a police lineup, how many of them could your key donors identify? I'm not suggesting that your ministry is populated with felons; I'm wondering how many of your donors have personal relationships with your leadership team. Donors should have a web of connections to your ministry, not know just one face.

A Friendship That Spans Two Thousand Miles

My mother is a committed Christian who has the spiritual gift of giving. She gives faithfully to her local church and donates to several ministries. Her gifts aren't at the six-figure level, but they are large enough to show up on a few ministry radar screens. Hers is an interesting case study in the best practices for cultivating donor relationships. A few ministries have her on their phone list and contact her regularly. Some ministry representatives know her by name, but the fascinating thing is that she knows many of them by name. Here's a rundown of her interactions (names changed):

1. "Ashley is just a phone representative who calls."
2. "Bryant wrote a thank you letter."
3. "Denise hasn't called me in a while."
4. "Two or three times Janet called me at mealtimes, and it annoyed me so much that I told her not to interrupt my dinner anymore." (When you're in your eighties, you value eating your dinner in peace! I guess that applies to people at any age.)
5. "I quit giving to Dr. Johnson (radio preacher). He's too old and just needs to quit."
6. "Grace's school (her great-granddaughter) wrote the nicest letter, but there was no receipt. I was confused, so I called them. They said that they sent the receipt in a separate letter."
7. "I get a form thank you letter from Truth Ministry. I know the president has had back problems."
8. "Michael wrote a personal thank you note, but he doesn't realize that I have macular degeneration and I have a difficult time reading his handwriting."
9. "Jack visits me occasionally."
10. "Faith Missions doesn't call."
11. "Neither does Hope House."
12. "Grace Outreach only sends a letter. They don't call."
13. "Someone from Global Ministry called and told me his name, but I don't remember it."
14. "Love Ministries has never contacted me."
15. "Barb calls to thank me and keep me updated about what's going on. I always enjoy talking with her. She knows about my health problems and always asks if there is anything she can pray for. Barb makes me feel like she knows me and that I'm important. Even though you might be two thousand miles away, you feel that you know one another."

Scan down through the list. Some ministries are developing deep relationships with their donors, others are ignoring them. Which of these ministries do you think will move up the list and which ones could drop off?

Everybody in the church at Rome knew the apostle Paul's name, but amazingly, he knew their names. In Romans 16, he greeted more than thirty people by name. These friends were co-laborers in ministry with Paul, and he was grateful for the many ways each one had helped him. To Paul, the church in Rome wasn't just a faceless, nameless donor. It was his family filled with brothers and sisters, fathers and mothers, whom he knew and loved. As an executive director, board member, or staff person, you should strive to develop these types of deep relationships. Making a thank you phone call will take you one step closer.

> How many of your donors have personal relationships with your leadership team?

Thanks, but No Thanks

Jeff is a college student who was planning to take a mission trip to Guatemala. He sent a form letter to a donor asking for support, and the donor responded with a generous gift. Jeff went on his trip and evidently had a great time. I said "evidently," because he never shared with the donor what happened on his trip. A year later, God moved in Jeff's heart to take a mission trip to Peru. This time he called his donor friend and started his conversation with, "First, I want to thank you for your gift for my Guatemala trip." And in the very next breath he said, "This year, I want to go to Peru and was wondering if you would be interested in supporting me." Jeff's past benefactor was gracious, but he graciously declined. Unfortunately, Jeff had to learn a valuable lesson the hard way: Thank you has an expiration date. We can chalk up this missed opportunity to youth and inexperience, but surprisingly, many Christian organizations are making the same mistake.

Thankfulness might seem like an insignificant gesture in charitable giving, but it can make all the difference in the world. Don't be one of the nine out of ten organizations that hurry off to enjoy a gift. Take the time to genuinely express your appreciation. You'll be glad you did.

Colin Smith—It's for You

Colin Smith is the Senior Pastor of the Orchard Evangelical Free Church in Illinois. Like every mega-church senior pastor, Colin juggles a busy schedule. But he's not too busy to thank those who partner with him. Remember the list of ministries that reached out to my mom? One of them was Colin's radio ministry. Barb usually calls from *Unlocking the Bible* to thank Mom for her gifts, but one evening when she picked up the phone Mom heard, "Hello, this is Colin Smith." At first she thought it was a recorded message, but he assured her that it was really him. He thanked her for her support and shared an update about the ministry. She was so impressed that he would take the time to call. I emailed Colin to thank him for calling my mom and to learn about his fundraising experiences. Colin is immersed in fundraising because his church is in a $15 million campaign, and he also participates in the ongoing fundraising efforts for his radio ministry.

Do you approach fundraising in your church differently than for your radio ministry?

I have chosen to be blind to what people give in my congregation. Others might do it differently, but that's what seems most comfortable for me and the culture of our church. For our church campaign, I share our church's vision from the pulpit, at town hall meetings, in small group presentations, and in personal conversations. I generally don't know what someone commits to our campaign, but if I have asked someone directly to consider a gift, many times they will tell me the amount God is leading them to give. When it comes to radio donors, my main interaction with them is through handwritten thank you notes and phone calls. I meet with a few radio partners personally. For all of our radio donors, I have full knowledge of their giving history.

What strategies do you use in your church's capital campaign?

Our leadership team started with prayer and fasting to ask God how to involve our people. We decided that the best approach would be to share the vision in small group settings. We invite twelve to fifteen people to someone's home to talk about where we are as a congregation, where we believe God is leading, and how we are going to get there. I answer questions and ask everyone to consider how God might be challenging them to participate in our campaign. Our campaign director then makes follow-up visits to answer any additional questions and ask for financial commitments.

Do you make donor thank you calls on a regular basis?

I try to set aside one night per week for pastoral work. I don't make a distinction between fundraising and pastoral ministry. I see it as all part of the same work. Some of my calls are simply to encourage people in our congregation; some are to thank our radio friends. I spent most of last evening making calls and writing notes. One was to a couple in our church who lost a loved one a few weeks ago. I called to encourage and pray with them. Then I wrote to a longtime radio listener. The husband is eighty-seven years old, and his wife is ninety. She has been blind for several years, and they listen to the broadcast every day. We are currently involved in a Vietnamese translation project, and I called to thank them for making it possible. I approach donor relationships with a pastor's heart. Reaching out to people is not just about money. If I made it only about money, I would dry up.

Do you have a system for your thank you strategy?

There's an element of randomness with my personal thank you calls, but there is also an element of structure. A few years ago we organized a team of lay volunteers who regularly phone our radio listeners. Our plan is to call everyone who purchased a resource and ask if the CDs are helpful. The team also calls to thank donors for their generous support. We always ask for prayer requests and offer to pray. People respond very positively. They might share some health concern or that their son or daughter is not a believer. We pray for these requests. Our volunteers love calling because they are reaching out to old friends and making new friends. Occasionally, we will call and ask for a gift.

Share a blessing from a thank you call.

There are so many stories of people who have been touched by the ministry and then respond with a gift. Carl is one of my special friends in Iowa. He was going through a difficult time and was ready to leave his second wife. One day he was listening to a sermon in his car and gave his heart to the Lord. He was miraculously born again. Three years ago God restored his marriage. It's a wonderful story of redemption. Every time I talk with him, it's a cherished conversation. These thank you calls don't follow an impersonal phone script; it's fellowshipping with friends to hear what the Lord is doing in their lives. It's not structured; it's just life.

How do you cultivate deeper relationships with members in your congregation?

As a leadership team, we ask ourselves how we can engage more with the circle of people in our church who give significantly. I like to meet informally with core people to share how God is working and ask for their input for what we are missing. We have perceptions of how we are doing, but it's so important to listen to honest feedback from those who are committed to the ministry. These meetings aren't about asking for money but for sharing our vision. I have higher levels of conversation with a few of our key supporters because we are involved in ministry together. Recently, I had breakfast with a generous donor. We didn't talk about money but about how we can motivate our people to buy into the vision. At the end of our conversation I said to him, "I can't thank you enough for everything you do and every way you serve the Lord here. You are right in the middle of what's going on." Fundraising is so much deeper than just asking for money; it's about building lifelong relationships.

> Fundraising is so much deeper than just asking for money; it's about building lifelong relationships.

Thanks again for calling to thank my mom!

I remember that conversation with your mom. We had a wonderful time. It took her a while to believe it was me. You are blessed to have such a godly heritage.

Action Step 7: Thank

Group Discussion

1. **Our attitude toward thankfulness can be characterized as:**
   - ❏ Stone Cold
   - ❏ Cool Ashes
   - ❏ Burning Embers
   - ❏ Raging Fire

2. **Do we know what thank you strategies our ministry has in place? If not, why not? If so, what are they?**

   _____

   _____

3. **What are we doing right in our thank you strategy that we could amplify?**

   _____

   _____

4. **What's missing in our thank you strategy that we could add?**

   _____

   _____

5. **Are there any barriers keeping us from implementing a board thank you call strategy? If so, what are they?**

   _____

   _____

Personal Reflection

Will I volunteer to make thank you phone calls?

CONCLUSION

You Have Not, because You Ask Not

A missionary in Central Asia took his family for a hike in the countryside and walked by a rock foundation of an abandoned building. He noticed two ten-year-old boys playing on top of the wall, but there didn't seem to be any easy way to scale the wall. So he asked, "How did you boys get up there?" One of them simply said, "He pushed me and I pulled him." That's a pretty good strategy for rock climbing, and it's also a great lesson for fundraising.

Fundraising is a team sport. It might seem that fundraising superstars can single-handedly raise millions of dollars, but most successful fundraising efforts require a team of committed individuals. Fundraising is based on relationships, so everyone in your organization needs to help identify, cultivate, and solicit donors. New major donors get interested in your ministry because they are friends with a trustee, member of your staff, volunteer, or even another donor. Some of the best connections might even come through the individuals you serve.

While it's great to have everyone's radar tuned to major donors, typically, if it's everybody's job, it's nobody's job. Practically speaking, fundraising falls on the executive director and board members. So like it or not, fundraising is a major part of your job description.

The Power of Two

Solomon understood the value of teamwork. "Two are better than one, because they have a good return for their labor: If either of them falls down, one can help the other up. But pity anyone who falls and has no one to help them up" (Eccl. 4:9–10). Many executive directors are forced to take on the lion's share of fundraising with little or no support from their board members. Unfortunately, that becomes an unsustainable scenario because the burdens of raising money are too heavy for one person to carry alone.

Even if you don't have the luxury of a development staff or engaged board members, you still need to find a fundraising buddy. Moses needed Joshua, Paul needed Barnabas, and Jeremiah needed Ebed-Melek. Not familiar with old E.M.? He played a very important role in Jeremiah's life. The prophet was faithfully warning Israel to turn from their wicked ways. Sadly for Jeremiah, some in his audience got tired of listening to him and threw him down a cistern to rot. He would have died there, but his friend Ebed-Melek came to his rescue. He grabbed a rope and thirty of his closest friends, and they hoisted Jeremiah up out of the muck (see Jer. 38:1–13).

If you've been involved in fundraising for any length of time, you probably have spent some time in the "pit of despair." People don't return your phone calls. When you do catch them on the phone, they politely decline your invitation to meet with them personally. Sometimes even your faithful donors don't seem interested in getting more involved. You need a fundraising friend to lift you up when your spirits sink into the mud. Solomon realized that, "Though one may be overpowered, two can defend themselves. A cord of three strands is not quickly broken" (Eccl. 4:12). Find a fundraising buddy. Better yet, find two.

A Little Push

Your fundraising friends can encourage you when you get discouraged, but they also provide the accountability you need to stay on task. Executive directors often succumb to the tyranny of the urgent and can become easily distracted putting out fires. Fundraisers are motivated by one of two realities: you either "have to" or you "want to." Board members usually provide the "have to" kick in the pants, but fundraising buddies can turn raising money into a "want to" activity.

So you're thinking to yourself, "I'd love to have a partner who would help me fundraise, but when I ask for volunteers, I just get blank stares." Okay, your team might be a little weak, but you don't need twenty-five fundraising superstars, you just need two or three who are willing to learn with you. If you don't have anyone who can encourage you, look for someone you can encourage. Recruit a friend who is passionate about your ministry and will join you on this fundraising journey.

> Fundraisers are motivated by one of two realities: you either "have to" or you "want to."

In many ways fundraising is similar to evangelism. Some people have the gift of evangelism and start sharing their faith immediately after they trust Christ. Others find it more difficult, but we are all called to spread the good news. Whether or not you're gifted in fundraising, you need to learn how to raise more money. How did you learn to share your faith? Perhaps you read a book, took a class, or maybe you even attended a seminar. Those activities can be helpful, but the best way to learn how to share your faith is to go with someone and experience sharing with them. That's also the best way to learn fundraising. Go visit a major donor with your fundraising buddy and learn to ask together.

The Next "History's Handful"

Bill Bright's concept of engaging donors in the work of the ministry still works today. John Maisel has an unquenchable zeal for evangelism. He spent his early ministry years making trips behind the Iron Curtain to share Jesus Christ. In 1993, he founded East-West Ministries International to train national pastors to become catalysts for indigenous church growth. John's driving passion is to energize the church in America for evangelism, so he started taking businessmen with him on evangelistic trips to a limited access country in Latin America. For many of these men, this was their first cross-cultural experience, and for some it was the very first time they had shared their faith. East-West partners with national churches to line up evangelistic calls, and then the team spends a week going from house to house with a church worker sharing the gospel through a translator. God continues to bless this outreach. Thousands of souls have come to Christ because of their witness.

But the real transformation was in the hearts of those businessmen who went on these trips. Some who were tentative about sharing their faith became bold and courageous evangelists. Not only did they grow in their faith, they developed close personal relationships with John and the East-West team. God gave these men a heart for reaching the lost, and he also gave them a heart for generous giving so that others can reach the lost. For these major donors, giving to East-West isn't just a transaction; it represents a transformation!

How can your ministry raise up a handful of key donors who will partner with you? It all starts with building personal relationships. John Maisel has been involved in two to three Bible studies with businessmen each week for more than twenty years, plus five to six one-on-one meetings each week. One executive said, "I know that John cares more about my spiritual life than any amount of money I could give to the ministry." Maisel, as his friends affectionately call him, develops "iron sharpening iron" relationships with men and isn't afraid to challenge them. (One time he tore up a person's check because he was giving for the wrong reasons.) As a result, a handful of godly men stand up and say, "John can ask me for anything, and I will do it."

> How can your ministry raise up a handful of key donors who will partner with you? It all starts with building personal relationships.

Final Thoughts

You and your ministry are living in one of two verses. You are either experiencing James 4:2, "You do not have because you do not ask God," or you are enjoying the blessings of Matthew 7:8, "For everyone who asks receives; the one who seeks finds; and to the one who knocks, the door will be opened."

Review these action steps one more time.

🙏	**Action Step 1:** **Pray**	Raising money for Christian endeavors must be a spiritual activity for the asker and the donor.
	Action Step 2: **Give**	You must give a generous, sacrificial gift before you can ask others to support your ministry.
	Action Step 3: **Network**	Fundraising is not about what you know but who you know.
	Action Step 4: **Invite**	The most effective way to build a donor base is one friend at a time.
	Action Step 5: **Ask**	Perhaps the most fearful step of all is to ask someone for money.
	Action Step 6: **Work**	Nothing's easy! Successful fundraising requires relentless patience and hard work.
	Action Step 7: **Thank**	It doesn't cost much to say thanks, but it might cost a lot if you forget to do it.

Now go ask for a fish!

Bringing It Home

Group Discussion

1. **Our board's passion for this ministry can be characterized as:**
   - ☐ Stone Cold
   - ☐ Cool Ashes
   - ☐ Burning Embers
   - ☐ Raging Fire

2. **How can we develop our own "History's Handful"?**

   _____

   _____

3. **How can we convert our donors from spectators to participants?**

   _____

   _____

4. **Can we organize a vision trip to involve donors? If so, how? When?**

   _____

   _____

5. **How can we make a spiritual impact on individual donors?**

   _____

   _____

Personal Reflection

How am I a champion for this ministry?

NOTES

[1] J. G. Turner, *Bill Bright and Campus Crusade for Christ: The Renewal of Evangelicalism in Postwar America* (Chapel Hill, NC: The University of North Carolina Press, 2008), 173–198.

[2] G. Müeller, *Answers to Prayer, moodyclassics.com*: www.moodyclassics.com: http://moodyclassics.com/?p=4, accessed January 15, 2013.

[3] Ibid.

[4] Corporation for National and Community Service (2012). *"Volunteering and Civic Life in America 2012"* http://www.volunteeringinamerica.gov/assets/resources/factsheetfinal.pdf, accessed January 7, 2013.

[5] BoardSource (2007). *The Challenges of Board Recruitment.* Retrieved from www.boardsource.org: http://www.boardsource.org/Spotlight.asp?ID=116.399, accessed December 17, 2012.

[6] *Facebook Claims 4.74 Degrees of Kevin Bacon* (2011, November 22). Retrieved from www.foxnews.com: http://www.foxnews.com/tech/2011/11/22/facebook-claims-474-degrees-kevin-bacon/#ixzz1eSOt5fTX, accessed November 3, 2012.

[7] J. Carver, *Boards that Make a Difference: A New Design for Leadership in Nonprofit and Public Organizations, second edition* (San Francisco, CA: Jossey-Bass, 1997), 133.

[8] www.rubegoldberg.com, accessed December 14, 2012.

BOARD RESOURCES

Board Member Self-Evaluation

A-Raging Fire   **B-**Burning Embers   **C-**Cool Ashes   **D-**Stone Cold

1.	**Prayer.** I pray regularly for this ministry, its board, staff, and especially the executive director.	A B C D
2.	**Testimony.** I demonstrate a positive Christian witness in my life and vocation.	A B C D
3.	**Church Involvement.** I participate regularly in worship and community in my local church.	A B C D
4.	**Board Attendance.** I have faithfully attended the board and committee meetings.	A B C D
5.	**Giving.** I give generously to this ministry, in proportion to my ability, demonstrating a high priority to this ministry.	A B C D
6.	**Agreement.** I have signed, and am in full agreement with, the Statement of Faith.	A B C D
7.	**Involvement.** Based on my understanding of what is expected of me in volunteer roles outside of my board responsibilities, I have served effectively.	A B C D
8.	**Knowledge.** I have remained informed about this ministry by regularly reading its publications, brochures, board reports, and other materials sent to me.	A B C D
9.	**Networking.** I have encouraged my friends and acquaintances to participate in this ministry as donors, volunteers, or in other ways.	A B C D
10.	**Wisdom.** I have provided advice, counsel, effective decision-making, feedback, and evaluation to the board and/or executive director.	A B C D

Sample Board Member Statement of Agreement

As a board member of ABC Ministry, I understand that my duties and responsibilities include the following:

1. **I am spiritually responsible** for this ministry and will seek God's wisdom for every decision. I pledge to keep this organization focused on glorifying God in everything that we do.

2. **I am fiscally responsible,** with the other board members, for this organization. It is my duty to know what our budget is, to be active in planning that budget, and participate in the fundraising efforts to meet that budget.

3. **I will give** what for me is a generous, sacrificial gift. I may give this as a one-time donation each year, or I may pledge to give a certain amount several times during the year.

4. **I will actively engage in fundraising** for this organization in whatever ways are best suited to me. These may include personal solicitation, assisting with special events, writing mail appeals, or thanking donors. I am making a good faith agreement to do my best to bring in as much money as I can.

5. **I am legally and ethically responsible,** along with the other board members, for this organization. I am responsible to know and approve all policies and programs, and to oversee their implementation. I know that if I fail in my tasks, and if the organization becomes the subject of a suit from a private person, or from the federal or state government, I may be held personally liable for the debts incurred.

6. **I will make every effort to attend** every board meeting, as well as the meetings of each Board committee on which I agree to sit. I understand that serving as a board member requires a significant time commitment, perhaps five to ten hours per month.

7. **I understand that no quotas have been set,** or no rigid standards of measurement and achievement have been formed. We trust each other to carry out these agreements to the best of our ability, each in our own way, with knowledge, approval and support of all. I know that if I fail to act in good faith, I should resign, or the board may ask me to resign.

In turn, ABC Ministry is responsible to me in a number of ways:

1. **I will be sent** regular financial and program reports, without having to request them, and will receive a draft annual budget for review prior to the meeting at which it is discussed and approved.

2. **I will be kept informed** about the progress and problems of the organization, and will receive accurate, complete, and timely information about any issues or problems that may have a major impact upon the organization, its staff, or board.

3. **I can call** the board chair and the executive director to discuss overall programs and policies. I can also ask the management staff to answer questions or concerns I might have regarding my committee responsibilities.

4. **Board members and staff** will respond with openness and transparency to any questions I have which I feel are necessary to carry out my spiritual, legal, or fiscal responsibilities.

5. (If applicable) ABC Ministry will maintain **Directors and Officers insurance** to limit my legal liability, and the executive director will maintain appropriate financial, personnel, and other management systems and procedures to minimize the possibility of legal or financial challenges.

Signed _____

Date_____

Adapted from *The Nonprofit Policy Sampler, Second Edition* by Barbara Lawrence and Outi Flynn, a publication of BoardSource, formerly the National Center for Nonprofit Boards. For more information about BoardSource, call 800-883-6262 or visit www.boardsource.org. BoardSource © 2006.

Services offered by The Timothy Group

Annual Fundraising
Capital Campaigns
Church Stewardship Campaigns
Development Assessments
Development Staff Training
Estate and Gift Design
Executive Searches
Feasibility/Pre-Campaign Studies
Film & Video Production
Focus Groups
Foundation Grant Seeking
Foundation Research
Graphic Design
Major Donor Programs
Phonathons
Print & Electronic Media
Professional DynaMetric Programs®
Public Relations
Special Events
Strategic & Long Range Planning

the**TIMOTHY**group
VISION. EXPERIENCE. LEADERSHIP.

1663 Sutherland Dr SE
Grand Rapids, MI 49508
616-224-4060
www.timothygroup.com

 Subscribe to our YouTube Channel

 Find me on Linkedin

 Follow us on Twitter

 Like us on Facebook

Are you ready to learn more about asking for a major gift?

Then you must read...

Pat McLaughlin is the president and founder of The Timothy Group. His time-tested, biblical fundraising methods have helped clients achieve their funding goals and build life-long relationships with major donors.

Winning with your major donors starts with a great game plan and team. It's not rocket science, it's all about relationships. Major Donor Game Plan outlines 6 R's for identifying, cultivating, and soliciting major donors.

Research. Who do you know? Look closer at current donors, past donors, lapsed donors, friends of board members, friends of donors, volunteers, and generous people in your community that share your values.

Romance. Cultivate relationships with these donors. Visit them in their homes or offices, take them out to breakfast or lunch, send them handwritten notes, and give them a tour of your ministry.

Request. Approach your donors with your needs. Major donors want to know what you want from them. You must ask.

Recognize. Genuinely say, "Thank you." It's time well invested.

Recruit. Find new donors. Major donors know other major donors. Ask those who have given to introduce you to others who may be interested.

Report. Communicate regularly with your donors and share with them how their gifts are making an eternal impact.

The principles shared in Major Donor Game Plan can make an immediate impact on your annual, capital and endowment funding needs.

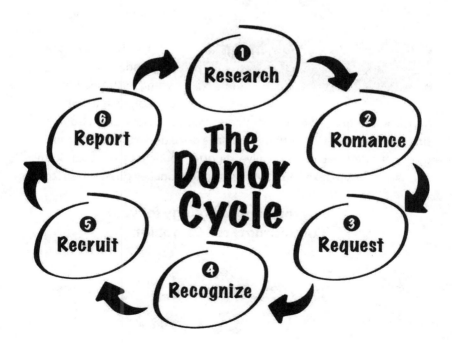

Before you launch your next capital campaign, you must read...

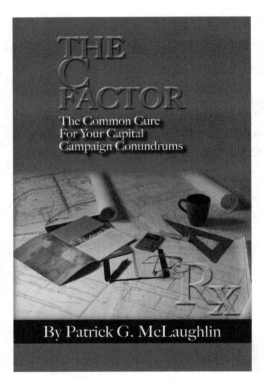

Murphy must have chaired a capital campaign because his law describes many fundraising efforts, "Anything that can go wrong will go wrong." The C Factor provides a biblically-based, theoretically-sound framework for conducting a successful capital campaign. Learn how to avoid common capital campaign conundrums whether you're in the planning stages a campaign, or in the middle of a campaign that is veering off track.

Yogi Berra once said, "We made too many wrong mistakes." Too many campaigns start with high hopes only to bog down with strategies that don't work. Learn from the successes and failures of others who have gone down the capital campaign road before. Discover twelve important principles for conundrum-free campaigns to take your ministry through four key phases to success.

Follow this simple strategy for your Conundrum Free Campaign:

RX + **Diagnosis.** Start with an accurate assessment of your current reality.

 DR + **Donor Research.** Uncover the human and financial resources you will need before you launch your campaign.

 GP + **Good Plan.** The right strategies, organizational structure, and campaign counsel will make the difference between your success or potential failure.

 CV + **Committed Volunteers.** When volunteers are motivated to give and encourage others to give, your campaign will take great strides forward.

 HW + **Hard Work.** Successful campaigns don't just happen. They require the focus and energy of the executive director, board members, staff, and key volunteers.

 PG **Power of God.** "Unless the Lord builds the house, the builders labor in vain" (Psa. 127.1).

 =CFC **Conundrum Free Campaign!**

The C Factor will equip you with "how to" direction for your campaign. These are not hypothetical strategies ready for a field test, but tried-and-true methods that can help you avoid the big mistakes and seize the opportunities that lie before you.

Want to learn more about biblical stewardship? Then you must read...

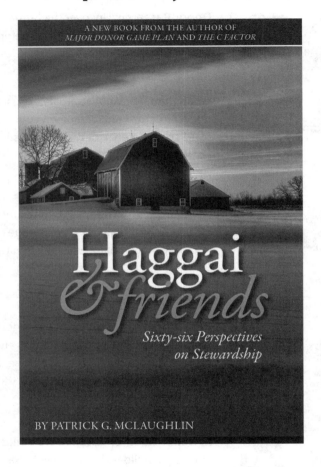

C. I. Scofield said it well, "Stewardship cannot be faked. Our checkbook defines our stewardship," and "Don't show me (the) tattered and worn pages of a man's Bible, show me a man's checkbook and therein lie his priorities."

Stewardship is a term that is often misused and misunderstood. Pat takes a fresh approach to biblical stewardship by considering what it means to become an "Obedient Owner." Haggai challenged Israel five times to "Give careful thought to your ways" (Hag. 1:5). The people in

Haggai's day fell into the same trap that many Christians do today. They were more concerned with enjoying life and all their possessions than using their resources to advance God's kingdom. Pat explores all sixty-six books of Scripture to discover a stewardship component from Genesis to Revelation.

Haggai's message is relevant to modern day Christians and his five probing questions are worth our consideration:

1. Have I planted much, but harvested very little?
2. Do I eat, but never seem to have enough to satisfy?
3. Am I always thirsty even though I have plenty to drink?
4. Do I have nice warm clothes, but always seem to be under-dressed and cold?
5. Do I make good or at least decent money, but put it into a wallet with holes?

From the foot of the cross, to the foot of the throne every decision is a stewardship decision. Stewardship is more than money, it's everything we do and say after we believe. Haggai & Friends is a major lesson from a minor prophet that will challenge you to rethink, renew, or redo your practice of biblical stewardship.

Don't Store Up Treasures